PRAISE FOR *HOW TO LIVE FOREVER*

"In this powerful and persuasive work, Marc Freedman shows that the generation gap is far from inevitable. In its place, he offers a compelling vision for the future of intergenerational relations: an alliance of talents that brings joy, empowerment, and abundance to both youth and old age. *How to Live Forever* is a heartfelt and heartwarming book that will spark purpose in the young and hope in their elders."—**Daniel H. Pink**, author of *When* and *Drive*

"Twenty years ago I read Marc Freedman's groundbreaking book *Prime Time* and it changed my life . . . inspiring and guiding me as I embarked on my encore career. With *How to Live Forever*, Freedman has done it again. This extraordinary, insightful, and deeply moving book will touch your heart and remain on your mind long after you put it down. It might even change your life!"—**Sherry Lansing**, former chairman and CEO of Paramount Pictures and founder and CEO of the Sherry Lansing Foundation

"Marc Freedman knows that we owe our kids more—more caring adults, more support, more hope, more love. And he knows that we have the human beings—tens of millions of us over fifty—who can deliver. If you care about kids, read this beautiful, hopeful book, get swept away by the power of its argument and its stories, and step up to the challenge. Surely, our generation can do more to change the odds."—**Arne Duncan**, former US Secretary of Education and author of *How Schools Work*

"Marc Freedman has written a warm, personal and inspiring alternative to the sorry national narrative of generational conflict. This is an important bookend to Atul Gawande's *Being Mortal* and a humane guide to true immortality."—**Ellen Goodman**, Pulitzer Prize–winning columnist, author, and founder of the Conversation Project

"Marc Freedman's *How to Live Forever* not only makes a compelling case for why it is imperative that we unite people of all ages across a shared vision, but it lays out specifically how older Americans can find purpose and happiness later in life. This is a must-read for anyone interested in creating a more inclusive and unified society for future generation CEO of the Walt Disney Company and foun

"*How to Live Forever* is a beautiful guide for helping all of us embrace the journey of life and contribute all we can at each stage. I'm so grateful to Marc Freedman for sharing this vision of a society that values and maximizes everyone, young and old."—**Wendy Kopp**, founder of Teach For America and CEO of Teach For All

"'Live mortal,' Marc Freedman advises: accept aging, build meaningful relationships with people of all ages, age-integrate *everything*—and get cracking. That's how to build the multigenerational world we all hope to live long enough to inhabit and, in the process, create legacies that outlive us. This deeply optimistic book is Freedman's legacy, and what a gift."—**Ashton Applewhite**, author of *This Chair Rocks: A Manifesto Against Ageism*

"Marc Freedman is today's most insightful thinker about thriving in the second half of life. With personal stories and robust science, *How to Live Forever* argues that finding meaning is the surest way to happiness, and that investing in the young—rather than competing with them—is the best route of all. Anyone over forty will love this witty, humble, compelling, and most of all, hopeful, book."—**Barbara Bradley Hagerty**, *New York Times* bestselling author of *Life Reimagined*

"Forget skin creams and fad diets. As Marc Freedman reminds us, there is only one way to live forever: be useful to others—especially to those coming up behind you. In this wise, inspiring, and practical book, he offers us all a clear path to a purposeful life."—**Eric Liu**, CEO of Citizen University and author of *You're More Powerful Than You Think*

"A beautifully written, often funny, and deeply moving guide to finding purpose and joy in the second half of life, *How to Live Forever* is a blueprint for making the most of our multigenerational future. I loved this book and you will, too."—**Henry Timms**, cofounder of #GivingTuesday and coauthor of *New Power*

"In this wonderful, insightful and above all inspiring book, Marc Freedman reminds us that longer lives aren't just about retirement income, keeping fit and the golf course but about engagement and connectivity—connecting together the different stages of your own life and connecting people at different stages of life. With humanity and wisdom, Freedman offers a positive view of aging and life's journey and how as an individual and as a society we should relish the opportunity"—**Andrew Scott**, Professor of Economics, London Business School, and coauthor of *The Hundred Year Life*

"Longevity is humanity's new frontier, and Marc Freedman is one of its greatest explorers. In *How to Live Forever*, he charts a path to improved relationships between young and old while providing a cornucopia of ideas for personal reinvention. This is the book we've all been waiting for."—**Ken Dychtwald, PhD**, author of *Age Wave* and *A New Purpose: Redefining Money, Family, Work, Retirement, and Success*

"This moving, thoughtful book is perfect for all of us who crave more meaning and connection as we age. Highly recommended!"—**Dan Heath**, coauthor (with Chip Heath) of *Switch* and *The Power of Moments*

"Part surprising history, part fascinating sociology, part inspiring manifesto— you close Freedman's book feeling determined to end age segregation, and better yet, crystal clear on how to do just that."—**Courtney E. Martin**, author of *The New Better Off: Reinventing the American Dream*

"One of the best books by a social observer or social entrepreneur I've ever read! Filled with wonderful writing, smart observations, humor, humility, and humanity, *How to Live Forever* will make you hopeful about our individual and collective futures."—**John Gomperts**, CEO of America's Promise Alliance

"*How to Live Forever* isn't just the best-ever title for a book. Marc Freedman has given us an entirely new way to think about our common future, along with tips we can all use to leave an enduring legacy."—**Sree Sreenivasan**, former chief digital officer of New York City, the Metropolitan Museum of Art, and Columbia University

"What happens when people from different generations work and play and think together? Fresh ideas for tackling big societal problems, to start. But perhaps more importantly, Marc Freedman shows that intergenerational mixing can produce uniquely satisfying relationships for both the millennial and boomer alike. This book presents an inspiring vision for how we should each endeavor to reach up, across, and down the age bracket to form intergenerational friendships. They will enrich our lives and may even save the world."—**Ben Casnocha**, coauthor (with Reid Hoffman) of the number one *New York Times* bestseller *The Startup of You: Adapt to the Future, Invest in Yourself, and Transform Your Career*

"Lace up your hiking boots and embark on a path of discovery with Marc Freedman as he traverses the movement of older people connecting with younger ones. His message will motivate you to find 'purpose by investing in the next generation, forging a legacy that endures, and leaving the world better than we found it,' as he writes in this influential book. *How to Live Forever* is about possibilities and hope and dreams and, yes, stark reality, clearly voiced by someone I trust and admire, and you will too."—**Kerry Hannon**, *New York Times* columnist and author of *Great Jobs for Everyone 50+*

"Age is not just a number. It's a beckoning. In Marc Freedman's wonderful book, we meet scores of people who've discovered a passion and purpose in the second half of their lives by helping the young thrive. They needn't be marvelous outliers or heartwarming exceptions. They can be all of us."—**Paul Taylor**, author of *The Next America: Boomers, Millennials, and the Looming Generational Showdown*

"In a time of escalating social divides, it's not surprising that some forecast a future of intergenerational strife, an inevitable battle for resources and primacy. Marc Freedman sees it differently. In his latest and most compelling book, *How to Live Forever*, Freedman makes the case for generational interdependence—for the essential bond between old and young. For those in my generation, *How to Live Forever* is a call to action, offering powerful evidence that we can live more meaningful lives through connection with younger people and contribution to their health, education, and welfare."— **Paul Irving**, chairman of the Milken Institute Center for the Future of Aging

HOW TO LIVE
FOREVER

ALSO BY MARC FREEDMAN

The Big Shift: Navigating the New Stage Beyond Midlife

Encore: Finding Work that Matters in the Second Half of Life

Prime Time: How Baby Boomers Will Revolutionize Retirement and Transform America

The Kindness of Strangers: Adult Mentors, Urban Youth, and the New Voluntarism

HOW TO LIVE
FOREVER

THE ENDURING
POWER OF
CONNECTING THE
GENERATIONS

MARC FREEDMAN

PUBLICAFFAIRS
NEW YORK

PublicAffairs
Hachette Book Group
1290 Avenue of the Americas, New York, NY 10104
www.publicaffairsbooks.com
@Public_Affairs

Printed in the United States of America

First Edition: November 2018
First Trade Paperback Edition: December 2020

Published by PublicAffairs, an imprint of Perseus Books, LLC,
a subsidiary of Hachette Book Group, Inc. The PublicAffairs name and
logo is a trademark of the Hachette Book Group.

The Hachette Speakers Bureau provides a wide range of authors
for speaking events. To find out more, go to
www.hachettespeakersbureau.com or call (866) 376-6591.

The publisher is not responsible for websites (or their content)
that are not owned by the publisher.

Print book interior design by Amnet Systems.

Library of Congress Cataloging-in-Publication

Names: Freedman, Marc, author.
Title: How to live forever : the enduring power of connecting the generations
/ Marc Freedman.
Description: First edition. | New York, NY : PublicAffairs, [2018] | Includes
bibliographical references and index.
Identifiers: LCCN 2018030332 (print) | LCCN 2018032650 (ebook) | ISBN
9781541767799 (ebook) | ISBN 9781541767812 (hardcover)
Subjects: LCSH: Intergenerational relations. | Older people. | Youth.
Classification: LCC HM726 (ebook) | LCC HM726 .F74 2018 (print) | DDC
305.26--dc23
LC record available at https://lccn.loc.gov/2018030332

ISBNs: 978-1-5417-6781-2 (hardcover); 978-1-5417-6779-9 (ebook); 978-1-5417-6780-5 (paperback)

LSC-C

Printing 1, 2020

To Leslie and the kids,
June, Levi, and Micah

CONTENTS

FOREWORD

Spoiler alert: This book isn't really about how to live forever.

This book is about how your impact can live on forever, and that's something I think we all want.

Creating a legacy was already on my mind when, at nearly fifty years old, I sold my boutique hotel chain, Joie de Vivre. A couple of years later, I joined Airbnb as a mentor to its cofounder and CEO, Brian Chesky, and as head of global hospitality and strategy, reporting to Brian. (Yes, it's unorthodox to mentor your boss, but given that 40 percent of Americans now report to someone younger than them, we're likely to see more of this in the future.)

I'd never worked in a tech company before. I didn't read or write code. I was nearly twice the age of the average Airbnb employee, and I reported to a smart guy who was twenty-one years my junior and the CEO of the company. Brian had asked me to be his mentor, but I felt like an intern.

Modern Elder is the phrase I coined to mean both mentor and intern, student and sage. Modern Elders are coaches and collaborators, appreciated for their expertise and humility. Their curiosity opens up possibilities; their wisdom distills it.

Marc Freedman, one of the wisest thought leaders and most committed students in the aging and longevity world, has been my Modern Elder. This book is his masterpiece.

Marc popped up on my radar about ten years ago, even before I had an inkling of an interest in aging, longevity, or mentorship. The first thing I noticed when we met was just how generous he was with his time and attention, his contacts, and his optimism about what I was working on. And how sincere. Marc believes down to his toes in everything he does.

As I got to know Marc better, I began to see him as a beautiful alchemy of head and heart. He has a lot in his head, no question. No matter what topic I introduced, he was my librarian. At Airbnb, I was the librarian for all my younger colleagues. But in my conversations with Marc, whether we were talking about basketball or politics or longevity, he had the facts and the contacts at his fingertips and shared both freely. He's a mensch and a mentor—a mensch-tor, you might say. And there aren't too many of those in this world.

And then there's his heart. *How to Live Forever* is one of the most heart-centered books I've ever read. It's hard to read this book without getting choked up by Marc's superb and poignant storytelling. He has a gift for remembering and articulating details, conversations, and connections made across generations.

I'm drawn to this book, too, for its understanding of the power of intergenerational collaboration. For the first time, we're routinely seeing five generations in the workplace at the same time. That age diversity has huge potential value. There's growing evidence that age differences—in life experience, perspective, cultural framing, understanding of customers, even how the brain works—add up to smarter, more effective teams. And smarter, more successful organizations.

How to Live Forever is a soulful rallying cry for intergenerational collaboration like we've never seen before. Marc's optimism around a new generational compact, forged together and benefitting all, is more than inspiring. It's energizing. I finished this book brimming with optimism about our future. I hope you will, too.

If you're my age, chances are you may live another thirty or forty years. And, if you're anything like me, you likely want to live a life that is as rich and meaningful as it is long. If you keep your wisdom to yourself, it dies with you. But if you can lend your gifts of age to the next generation, that wisdom will never grow old.

I'm so grateful that Marc lent his wisdom to me—and to all of us—in this book. Its message will never grow old.

Chip Conley, 2020

Chip Conley is a New York Times*–bestselling author, most recently of* Wisdom at Work: The Making of a Modern Elder. *He is the founder of Joie de Vivre Hospitality and the Modern Elder Academy in Baja California Sur, Mexico, which he runs. He is a strategic adviser for hospitality and leadership at Airbnb and a board member at Encore.org.*

Introduction

EXTENSIONS

Getting things done on time has never been my strong suit. Twenty years ago I wrote my first book about getting older. The writing process, to say the least, was difficult. As the publisher's deadline neared, my anxiety became paralyzing. I spent day after day in front of a blank monitor, unshaven, pajama clad, increasingly disheveled, searching the web for distraction.

One day on a perverse whim, I went to Amazon and typed in the title of my book, only to discover that the manuscript I'd yet to start writing was already for sale. In a stupor of sleep-deprived insanity, I clicked the "Order Now" button. Maybe this was all a bad dream. If I selected overnight delivery, perhaps the next day I'd wake up to a UPS parcel rescuing me from the nightmare. The package never arrived.

I'm still not quite sure how that book got done. (Or this one, for that matter.) But I do know that my history of procrastination didn't start with these authorial woes.

I was already showing a talent in this area as an eighteen-year-old college freshman. In September of 1976, I drove ninety minutes from our house in Northeast Philadelphia to the leafy campus of Swarthmore College. I wasn't remotely ready for the rigors of higher education, especially those of the academic sweatshop my chosen institution would turn out to be.

The first in my family to attend such a demanding place, I was singularly unprepared. My father was a gym teacher turned school administrator, and my mother had gone to college for a year before dropping out. I attended a large, working-class public high school with six thousand students, including eighteen hundred in my graduating class. But I came of age at a time when even private higher education was far more accessible and affordable than it is today. My first year, the cost of tuition, room, and board at an Ivy League school or a private liberal arts college was about $6,000, total. Even kids like me whose parents didn't have the resources to help pay for a university education could scrape by on financial aid, work-study, and modest loans.

I was, from the outset, headed for failure. I tried basing my inaugural paper, "Introduction to the Old Testament," largely on the CliffsNotes edition for the Bible. My professor was unimpressed.

By the time I'd made it, academically bloodied and beaten, to the break between the semesters of my sophomore year, I had probably set something approaching an intercollegiate record for incomplete classes. I'd racked up nine by that point—impressive, if I do say so myself, considering that I'd only taken twelve courses and that four of them had been pass-fail.

As it turns out, there was a silver lining in all this failure. I desperately needed more time to finish assignments, and the school, in its wisdom, required only three steps to get an incomplete approved. The first was asking for one, the second was getting the professor to say yes, but the third required institutional approval, in the form of sign-off from the school's associate provost, an office held by a silver-haired, scraggly-bearded sixty-three-year-old named Gilmore Stott.

Gil Stott had himself come from modest means, something that likely contributed to his abundant empathy for struggling students like me. A kid from Indiana, he'd gone to the University of Cincinnati in the 1930s, excelling academically and earning a Rhodes Scholarship in part for completing a trans-Canadian canoe and bicycle trip with sausages tied to his back for sustenance.

During World War II, Stott served as an intelligence officer to General George Patton and fought in the Battle of the Bulge, winning the Bronze Star. This part is hard for me to imagine, given Stott's soft-spoken, utterly gentle demeanor, the opposite of Patton's blustering bravado. At Oxford's Balliol College, he studied philosophy, which led to a PhD from Princeton. After graduate school, Stott held positions in the Rhodes Scholarship organization and became the right-hand man to Frank Aydelotte, head of Princeton's famed Institute for Advanced Study during its heyday.

On the side, Gil served as Einstein's personal driver and confidant.

When Aydelotte became Swarthmore's president, Stott accompanied him, serving as an ethics professor and later as dean of admissions. He was a source of calm and a trusted bridge between groups during the turbulent times of the 1960s, when the college's charismatic president, Courtney Smith, died of a heart attack during a student takeover of the administration building. Gil chaired the Upward Bound program at the school, helping bring low-income students from nearby Chester to campus, where young people became acquainted with college life and received guidance to help prepare them for higher education.

A lifetime long-distance runner with a shockingly slow gait (it was almost like he was running in place), Stott was a thin, handsome man with smile lines at the corners of his eyes. I remember him clad in the tweed jacket you'd expect from a liberal arts college dean, along with an unexpected bolo tie, as if to say, "I'm not quite as buttoned down as you might think."

After my nine formal visits to his office to request incompletes, plus informal ones to request extensions of incompletes and more just to see the man, he took me under his wing, as did his grandmotherly administrative assistant, Etta Zwell. Together Stott and Zwell had a kind of Batman-and-Robin operation going, focused on bringing young people like me into the fold.

Whenever Gil could make out my slumped, dejected figure shuffling down the long corridor to his office with another request to buy some time on one course or another, he got a bemused smile on his face. He would grant me the extension, then invite me over for dinner—as would Etta. They became my family away from home, like surrogate grandparents.

As part of the extended Stott family, I was exposed to a whole new world for someone who had grown up in a Levittown-like housing development and gone to a vast, homogeneous high school. One summer, I traveled with Gary White, an African American student from Philadelphia and the center on the school's football team (the Little Quakers), to spend a week with the Stotts and other guests at their rustic retreat on Parry Island, several hours north of Toronto. For Gary and me, this was our first camping trip. On the way up, he taught me how to drive a stick shift.

Parry Island in the late summer was a shimmering vision of harmony, literally. Gil, a devoted cellist, and his violist wife, Mary, played in string quartets on the porch most evenings, accompanied by their violin-playing children—or one of the loose collection of students like me who were constantly coming and going. Back home, Gil and Mary age-integrated the college orchestra by joining it. According to his obituary, Gil added violin to his repertoire and took his last violin lesson the day before he died in 2005, at ninety-one.

For all his official roles at the college, Gil's truest title might have been tender of wayward students and their souls. The formal role he held mattered less than his eye for young people who were stumbling. And his main tools weren't advice and a wagging finger. He was a quiet man, so quiet that even if he was inclined to give advice, it might have been inaudible. What came across clearly was a blend of acceptance and love. Each of us felt that Gil was completely in our corner. And he was.

When I graduated, thanks in no small measure to Gil's support, I was elected to give the commencement address with my friend and former roommate Charlie McGovern. We dedicated the address to Gil, in part out of affection and also out of a sense that he wasn't fully given his due. We saw that despite Gil's importance in so many lives, he didn't have a fancy office or a lofty title.

In that concern, I think we were mistaken. Our dedication at graduation produced, to our surprise, a spontaneous, sustained, and thunderous standing ovation. A measure of the man's life. It was likewise a credit to the college's leaders that they recognized the value of such a role and provided the perch for Stott to carry it out while an employee and for two decades further after he "retired" in 1985. Today, a portrait of Gil Stott playing his beloved cello hangs in the entry of the main building of the college, in guardian angel–like fashion.

Still, even brilliant mentors can only do so much; I made a grammatical error in the first line of my speech.

KIDS VERSUS CANES?

Now I'm just about the age Gil was at the time we first met, which is remarkable to me. Then again, the idea that he would live thirty more years beyond his sixtieth birthday, twenty of them after formally retiring from the college, is testimony to the possibilities of extending life spans. Today, thanks to gains in longevity and the aging of the baby boom generation, ten thousand people turn sixty-five every day. By 2060, a quarter of the US population will be over sixty-five.

Perhaps even more significant, for the first time in our history, we now have more older people than younger ones. In 2016, for example, there were 110 million adults over fifty and only 74 million young people under eighteen, a trend that is here to stay.

The graying of America is understandably worrying for a country that has always prided itself on its youthful spirit and makeup. Academics and pundits alike predict that this demographic shift will have adverse effects on the prospects of young people, ushering in cross-generational conflict, zero-sum wrangling over scarce resources between "kids and canes," and a vast generation gap. Many worry about the so-called gray/brown divide, a gulf between a largely white older population and a much more diverse younger group.

Christopher Buckley provides a satirical solution to all these problems in his novel *Boomsday*—mass euthanasia for the gray-haired set, sending baby boomers off to the great beyond at seventy, to the betterment of all who remain. But even in the realm of satire, there's a glitch. A *New Yorker* cartoon depicts a pair of native Alaskans shaking their heads over a consequence of climate change—insufficient ice floes for dispatching the boomers.

The increase in the number of older people in America is paralleled by an increase in the needs of our kids. Today half of all public school students come from low-income families—and 80 percent of low-income kids aren't reading proficiently by the end of third grade. We're not making much of a dent in the child poverty rate or the educational achievement gap based on race and ethnicity. More children of color are getting to college, but not nearly enough are finishing. And social mobility is increasingly limited—42 percent of children born to parents in the lowest income bracket stay there as adults.

And yet we move forward as if our future weren't at stake. Those in power cut programs that feed, care for, and educate children; degrade the planet these young people will inherit; and saddle future generations with record debt. How can we find the will to realign priorities in a nation where children don't vote and older people do? Where are we going to find the resources, both human and financial, to cover the costs of an aging America and invest more in young people at the same time? If we don't, will we knowingly continue to sacrifice our children?

In 2014, two distinguished sixty-something boomers sounded the alarm. Stanley Druckenmiller and Geoffrey Canada embarked on a college tour not to figure out where to send their children but to alert young people that their futures were being compromised. The goal: to be modern-day Paul Reveres, waking up the next generation to the transgressions of their own.

The two crusaders were both students at Maine's Bowdoin College in the 1970s, although they didn't know each other at the time. Druckenmiller went on to generate a sizable fortune working with George Soros and then with his own firm, Duquesne Capital Management.

Canada made his mark creating the Harlem Children's Zone, one of the most successful and significant efforts to improve the lives of children (Druckenmiller served as the Children Zone's board chair). In 2009 the *Chronicle of Philanthropy* selected Druckenmiller as the most charitable man in the country.

Canada and Druckenmiller's 2014 *Wall Street Journal* op-ed setting out their argument, cowritten with Kevin Warsh, has a distinctly uncharitable title: "Generational Theft Needs to Be Arrested." In it, Canada and Druckenmiller indict the nation's growing debt burden, which "threatens to crush the next generation," along with entitlement programs that are "profoundly unfair to those who are taking their first steps in search of opportunity." The status quo, they write, is "tantamount to saddling school-age children with more debt, weaker economic growth, and fewer opportunities for jobs and advancement."

Thomas Friedman applauded the Druckenmiller-Canada tour in a *New York Times* column with an equally provocative title, "Sorry, Kids. We Ate It All." When the invariable senior citizen showed up at one of the duo's campus talks to protest that they were fomenting generational war, Friedman writes, Druckenmiller "has a standard reply. 'No, that war already happened, and the kids lost. We're just trying to recover some scraps for them.'"

Listening to Druckenmiller and Canada, and many other prominent figures heralding coming (or current) generational conflict, it's hard not to worry about how we'll ever survive the projected "gray dawn." Older voters dramatically outnumber younger ones at the polls today—and the two groups' interests can seem increasingly at odds. Indeed, it's possible to interpret developments like Brexit and the 2016 US presidential election as early indicators of the indifference of the old to the prospects of the young.

Demography is supposed to be destiny, and many believe the coming years will be full of animosity between generations. The perils are real, the fears and concerns legitimate. But I believe there's another way—and the possibility of a far better outcome, one that could help us avoid conflict, solve problems from literacy to loneliness, reweave the social fabric in communities, and reconnect us to our fundamental humanity.

BUILT FOR EACH OTHER

The route to this more uplifting prospect is neither obscure nor abstract. It's right in front of us, in everyday lived experience and common sense. Shift the currency from fiscal woes to emotional truths, and the result reveals something profoundly different—the needs and assets of the generations fit together like pieces of a jigsaw puzzle.

Let's start with families. There's probably no relationship more revered in modern life than the bond between grandparents and grandchildren. Indeed, a new book on the subject, Jane Isay's *Unconditional Love: A Guide to Navigating the Joys and Challenges of Being a Grandparent Today*, just arrived in my mailbox. I put it next to Lesley Stahl's *Becoming Grandma: The Joys and Science of the New Grandparenting* and several other recent volumes plumbing the depths of this bond. Stahl reports that "in various surveys, nearly three-quarters of grandparents say that being a grandparent is the single most important and satisfying thing in their life. Most say being with their grandkids is more important to them than traveling or having financial security."

Indeed, the presence and enthusiasm of grandparents often enriches the lives of older and younger people while making life easier and better for the generation in the middle, too. The *Economist* magazine, chronicling the wave of grandparents helping to support their grandchildren—in many cases, actually raising them—calls this fit between older and younger "the Silver-Haired Safety Net."

My wife, Leslie, and I have three sons, ages eight, ten, and twelve. (Yes, we got a very late start—sometimes I think we had our own grandchildren.) My own father, a doting grandparent, passed away this year, and my mother is both frail and twenty-five hundred miles away in Philadelphia. Leslie's mother, a healthy seventy, lives an eight-hour drive away and has eight grandchildren spread along the West Coast. It's a joyous occasion when she shows up to visit and help take care of the kids. But that happens two or three times a year at best, given the geographic distance and equitable distribution of grandparental love and assistance.

Still we've been fortunate. Our silver-haired safety net is located two doors down. Our quirky, engaging eighty-something neighbors, Jake and Joyce Anderson, have become quasi grandparents for our children, what anthropologists call "fictive kin." Their own grand-children live in Idaho and the Sierras, hours away. So they get to ply their grandparenting impulses on a day-to-day basis with our kids, and everybody is the better for it, especially our middle son, Levi, the maker in the family. He and Jake, a former aviation mechanic at the Alameda Naval Air Station, disappear on projects in Jake's toolroom, while our youngest son, Micah, a budding numismatist, spends time with Joyce going over her foreign coins.

When emergencies arise, we know we can count on Joyce and Jake to fill the void, offering the kids an occasional safe haven after school or coming by to help when there's a crisis. This all happens by virtue of proximity, but I suspect Jake and Joyce are a connection to a time when our block was a more communal one. They are also a connection to something deeper and more fundamental than the history of our neighborhood.

There is significant evidence from evolutionary anthropology and developmental psychology that old and young are built for each other. The old, as they move into the latter phases of life, are driven by a deep desire to be needed by and to nurture the next generation; the young have a need to be nurtured. It's a fit that goes back to the beginning of human history.

For many decades, evolutionary anthropologists tried to understand why women typically lived so long beyond reproductive age in the harsh world of the selfish gene. Men could continue reproducing late in life. But from a narrow evolutionary standpoint, postmenopausal women seemed superfluous—until an anthropologist from the University of Utah, Kristen Hawkes, developed the grandmother hypothesis, based on her research studying hunter-gatherer tribes in Tanzania and Paraguay. She found that older women played a critical role gathering food and caring for their daughters' children, thus enabling the longer gestational period that separates humans from most other species. In short, the role of grandmothers served as a critical missing link. If not for them, we likely wouldn't have evolved in the way we did or ended up living so long.

Alison Gopnik, a child psychologist at the University of California, Berkeley, argues that the evolutionary role of grandmothers in caring for children "may actually be the key to human nature." Meanwhile, Stanford psychologist Laura Carstensen, a preeminent scholar of later-life development, comes to similar conclusions about the grandmother hypothesis, arguing that older people are essential to future generations and the well-being of the species.

The echoes in the work of these two giants of developmental psychology who focus on opposite ends of the age spectrum are striking. After years of research, they came to similar conclusions about the essential connection between generations. So I asked Carstensen, a good friend, about the fit. She immediately raised an important question: Can the critical role of grandmothers and the benefits to children extend beyond the African savanna—and beyond older and younger people who are blood relations?

I wanted to know her take. "After so many decades of research on development across the life course," I asked her, "what do you think?" Carstensen's answer was immediate and affirmative. She described older people as a potential "cavalry coming over the hill" when it comes to meeting the needs of young people today. And she added that proximity is a key to realizing this promise. In other words, it helps to have a Joyce and Jake two doors down.

I know what she means. Older people—I should say "we"—often have the time and numbers. We have an impulse toward meaningful relationships that grows as we realize fewer days are ahead than behind. We have a deeply rooted instinct to connect in ways that flow down the generational chain. And we have a set of skills—patience, persistence, and emotional regulation, among others—that, study upon study shows, blossom with age. When it comes to cavalries coming over the hill, Carstensen points out, it's older people you want on those horses.

But, again, what does all this mean for us today, when gathering roots for grandchildren may not be the best and highest use of grandparent time? How can we tap the vast and largely underused talent of the older population (of men and women) to support the next generation in ways that fit contemporary realities? How can we do so within families but likewise across them and into the broader community?

In short, how can we adapt the grandmother hypothesis to the modern-family world?

THE RIPE MOMENT

There's evidence that the modern-family world may be ready. Despite all the negative headlines and kids versus canes rhetoric, polling shows remarkable warmth between the generations. Surveys reveal an extraordinary degree of mutual respect, most especially between boomers and millennials. And an overwhelming majority of older people say that the opportunity for future generations to prosper is important or very important to achieving America's promise, putting it on par with individual freedom, the work ethic, and free enterprise as priorities.

Attitudes are changing, but more importantly, behaviors are, too. We're witnessing an incipient movement today of older people who are connecting with younger ones, standing up and showing up for the next generation, and resisting the mandate to go off in pursuit of their own second childhood.

Instead of trying to be young, they're focused on being there for those who actually are.

I'll offer Stanley Druckenmiller as Exhibit A. The sixty-five-year-old investor has not only become a public voice for the next generation; he's helped spearhead a billion-dollar philanthropic fund, Blue Meridian Partners, to invest large sums in education and social programs for young people living in poverty.

And Druckenmiller is hardly alone. For more than thirty years, I've crisscrossed the country, meeting older people without Druckenmiller-sized bank accounts who are acting on the same desire, to leave the world better than they found it. And I've spent years—no doubt influenced by my experience with Gil Stott and a string of older mentors who followed—trying both to encourage this behavior and to create new ways for those in the second half of life to support younger people.

One of my inspirations is Cherry Hendrix, a woman I first met in 1986 in a Northeast Portland, Oregon, elementary school, in a rough-and-tumble neighborhood known for its high concentration of former inmates. Hendrix had moved to Portland from her native Alabama during World War II, part of the large migration of southern African American women to the ports and factories in the West and North. They came to support the war effort, and Cherry was, essentially, Rosie the Riveter.

After the war ended, Hendrix remained in Portland, managing a modest living until she retired at sixty and launched a second act in the Foster Grandparents program—a national vehicle for bringing more people over sixty into the lives of children from low-income backgrounds. When I met her, she'd been a foster grandparent for more than a decade, tutoring elementary school students for twenty hours a week in return for a small stipend.

The constraints of the tutoring relationship had gotten Hendrix thinking: How could she better connect with the children and gain their trust? An avid bowler, Cherry decided to start a bowling league for the kids. She talked to the management at Interstate Lanes in Portland, where she participated in a Jacks and Jills league. They agreed to provide shoes, gratis. Then the seventy-year-old woman handwrote forty-three permission slips for the children to bring home. Soon a thriving league was under way.

Hendrix, known as Grandma Cherry to the kids, would go on to become an inaugural member of Portland's Experience Corps—part of a national program I helped start (now run by AARP) that provides tutors and mentors who are over fifty to about thirty-one thousand children a year in 279 schools. Cherry "retired" from Experience Corps at the age of ninety-four and lived to ninety-nine, leaving five grandchildren, ten great-grandchildren, three great-great-grandchildren, and hundreds of other kids, now adults, whose lives she touched.

Women and men like Cherry Hendrix are doing a lot more than saving a few scraps from the table. They are deeply engaged in the lives of children, showing up day in and day out to provide caring, connection, and support. And they're getting an enormous amount out of these relationships themselves.

I know it's easy to dismiss Cherry Hendrix and others like her as marvelous outliers, heartwarming exceptions. But I'm convinced that these individuals are far from exceptions. They are the protagonists of another story, a tale of resilience that contrasts sharply with the zero-sum, old-versus-young, demography-as-despair narrative. It's a tale that is of growing significance today.

COMING FULL CIRCLE

This book is the chronicle of a nascent movement that has the potential to make the more-old-than-young world work, both for society and for individuals of all ages, not only right now but into the future. It's the story of Cherry Hendrix and so many others who are showing us the way forward, bringing into focus the power of older people investing in the next generation—and finding purpose, health, happiness, and even income while doing so. This book is an account of why their efforts matter, why they haven't yet realized their full potential as a movement, and what we can do to turn that around.

The stakes couldn't be higher as we choose between two paths forward, prompted by the new demographics and the arrival of our profoundly multigenerational future—one characterized by scarcity, conflict, and loneliness; the other by abundance, interdependence, and connection.

As you may have guessed, this account—this quest—is as personal as it is professional for me. Earlier this year, I turned sixty myself. If becoming a nation of more older people than younger ones is a shock to our national self-identity, I can say that crossing this Rubicon is a shock to my own self-conception. I was always the young person who admired and advocated for older people—at least that's how I saw myself.

This journey has been a surprise for me in more ways than one. I came to my vocation focused on kids, not older people. But I quickly discovered that the only resource big enough to help solve the problems facing the next generation is the older one. Back then, a world with more old than young seemed like a distant prospect. And I was a young person myself.

For the past three decades, I've worked to engage older people's untapped talents in helping to alleviate young people's unmet needs. This is an account of the lessons I've learned along the way, the older mentors who have supported me throughout, and my transformation from a younger person to one of them. Or, I should say, again, one of us.

In many ways the ensuing chapters are a sequel to *The Big Shift*, a book I wrote eight years ago to make the case that a new life stage is taking shape between the middle years and anything resembling true old age—a development akin to the creation of adolescence a hundred years ago. This emerging period has been described as "a season in search of a purpose." This book is about how we might find that purpose by investing in the next generation, forging a legacy that endures, and leaving the world better than we found it.

The humorist Fran Lebowitz has remarked that she always believed older people were a kind of ethnic group—that they had been born old! And that she was part of a different group, one born young. Until she realized that if we're lucky, we all become part of that seemingly other tribe.

Now that I'm here, I have so many more questions than answers. How will I go from being the recipient of love and support from a string of elders, starting with Gil Stott, to being one of the givers, a master of what matters? What lessons can I learn from the mentors I've been lucky enough to have? Can I be as good at giving as receiving? How does one make the time and the shift?

The ensuing chapters are as much about coming to grips with these personal questions as they are about wrestling with the question of how we make the most of a (much) older society. That's because, of course, the personal and societal questions are one and the same. How we answer will determine not only our collective ability to navigate the multigenerational world already upon us but also our individual ability to find the keys to happiness and fulfillment in the second half of life.

And the time for answers is now. No extensions allowed.

Chapter 1

BIOLOGY FLOWS DOWNHILL

"*The first person to live to 150 is alive today.*"

For months while commuting back and forth to work in rush-hour traffic, I found myself regularly stuck in front of a Prudential billboard proclaiming the world's first sesquicentenarian.

Prudential was hardly out to celebrate longer lives. Its goal, one can assume, was to shock and scare commuters into purchasing the company's retirement products. The tagline: "Let's get ready for a longer retirement."

With Prudential's website holding retirement age at 65 and its billboards proclaiming 150-year lives, the insurer seemed to be suggesting an 85-year version of the golden years, an endless end phase longer than the American life expectancy at the beginning of the twenty-first century.

The purported 150-year-old in the making was just the start. On my journey home, I ran a gauntlet of similar Prudential billboards, including this one: "1 in 3 Babies Born Today Will Live to be 100," followed by another tagline raising the specter of how much all of this was going to cost.

By the time I pulled into my driveway, I was suffering from the equivalent of postcommute longevity disorder, the warnings bouncing about my brain in pinball-like fashion. How were we ever going to pay for our exploding life spans? Who even wants to live to 150? Why is it that we are so obsessed with living so long?

LIFE EXTENSIONS

On February 21, 1963, President John F. Kennedy gave his most important speech on aging, stating that while we had added "years to life," it was time to add "life to those years." Since then, we've proven extraordinarily adept at the former, adding an average of almost two months a year to the American life span.

But we're still struggling to add purpose and engagement to the second half of life. A 2018 study from the Stanford University Graduate School of Education, in partnership with Encore.org, finds that nearly a third of older adults in the United States (31 percent) exhibit purpose beyond the self—that is, "they identify, prioritize, adopt and actively pursue goals that are both personally meaningful and contribute to the greater good." That's thirty-four million people over fifty, and it's very good news. The more troubling news: two-thirds of older adults in the United States don't yet have this kind of purpose in their lives.

Enter Silicon Valley. Not much interested in adding purpose to years and not content to add mere years (or even decades) to life, a handful of tech titans are on a crusade to radically extend longevity. Forget 150. That's early adolescence if the Silicon Valley set gets its way.

Some of the biggest and wealthiest names in technology are driving the frenzy around life extension. Alphabet, Google's parent, has teamed up with the French pharmaceutical company AbbVie to launch Calico with the goal of vastly extending life spans. X Prize founder Peter Diamandis and human genome sequencer Craig Venter formed Human Longevity with the same purpose in mind. The $1 million Palo Alto Longevity Prize is called simply a "science competition dedicated to ending aging."

And that's just the start. A cadre of tech titans has set its sights on the ultimate prize, ending mortality itself. PayPal cofounder Peter Thiel has declared himself opposed to death. "Basically, I'm against it," he said.

The media has joined the frenzy. *Forbes* ran a cover story in 2017 on "How to Cheat Death." *Time*'s headline: "Can Google Solve Death? . . . That Would Be Crazy—If It Weren't Google." Not to be outdone, *Bloomberg*'s story is titled "Google Wants You to LIVE FOREVER.*" The asterisk: "*Well, maybe just to 500."

Two of the leading proponents of endless life, scientists Ray Kurzweil and Aubrey de Grey, have a plan B—freezing themselves in liquid nitrogen if they end up at death's door before their predicted breakthroughs reach fruition. Kurzweil reportedly takes 150 supplements each day while drinking glass after glass of specially filtered water and visiting a clinic every week for chemical transfusions.

Today's forever-young entrepreneurs and activists lend themselves to easy lampooning. A 2017 episode of HBO's *Silicon Valley* parodied the vampire-like obsession with parabiosis, the process by which the blood of a young, healthy person is injected into that of an older one in an effort to preserve vitality. It's based on a century-old effort by a French scientist to fuse two mice, one old and the other young.

In the episode, Gavin Belson, cofounder of the fictional Google-esque company Hooli, is interrupted midmeeting by his "transfusion associate" Bryce, who barges into the conference room, wheeling a pair of throne-like chairs. Bryce—described by Gavin as looking like a Nazi propaganda poster—proceeds to plant himself in one of the chairs and begin pumping his strapping young blood into Belson.

The over-the-top parodies are often hard to distinguish from the immortalists' real-life grandiosity. Larry Ellison of Oracle has been quoted as saying, "Death has never made sense to me." (To which the critic Michael Kinsley quipped, "The question isn't whether death makes sense to Larry Ellison but whether Larry Ellison makes sense to death.")

Peter Thiel presents the prospects in apocalyptic, martial terms, describing "the vast forces of humanity in its titanic struggle against the Great Enemy of the world, whose true name is Death." He continues: "Death was natural in the past, but so was the instinct to fight it. The future only has room for one of them."

SOLVING THE WRONG PROBLEM

I understand the fear of death, having waited for enough medical test results and weathered my share of turbulence at thirty thousand feet. What's more, having had children late, I cross into my sixties with three boys twelve and under, who remind me daily how old I am. I may need parabiosis just to get them through high school.

Then there is the matter of death itself. My friend Ellen Goodman, founder of the Conversation Project, told me a joke about three old men in a bar, who are comparing what they want said at their funerals.

The first crows about being remembered for his vast business acumen, with colleagues rising to toast his commercial brilliance.

The second more humbly states that he wants to be eulogized for what a fine person he's been, a good father, husband, grandfather, and citizen.

The third, in disbelief, says he just wants three words uttered at his funeral: "Look—he's moving!"

Jokes and fears aside, Silicon Valley's death-cheating efforts amount to a colossal case of misplaced attention and resources, a cautionary tale reminding us to be careful what we wish for. The fundamental problem (all other problems aside) is that cheating death amounts to *cheating life*. It is one or the other, it seems to me: either radical life extension or continued reproduction for a planet straining at the seams to contain millions of new lives each year.

The Silicon Valley quest to extend life is the ultimate NIMBY (not in my backyard) project. Those who now inhabit the earth—let me be more specific, the 1 percenters who now inhabit the earth—simply refuse to cede it.

As medical ethicist Ezekiel Emanuel of the University of Pennsylvania sums things up, "With all these old Peter Thiels living on and on forever, the Earth would lack the carrying capacity for more people; there would be total resource limits precluding adding one more infant, much less the 130 million currently added each year. Maybe this is why the titans of technology want so badly to escape to Mars."

Emanuel himself has argued that he doesn't want to live past seventy-five, in part because having an end point is essential to living fully. Still he "retains the right" to change his mind when the three-quarter-century mark arrives.

Fortunately, little evidence exists that anyone, other than the small group of zealots leading this charge, really wants to live forever.

Nir Barzilai, a geneticist at Albert Einstein Medical College, offers an illustration. As reported in the *New Yorker*, Barzilai screened a documentary on longevity for an audience of a few hundred individuals. After showing the film, the scientist conducted an informal experiment with the group in attendance: "I said, 'In nature, longevity and reproduction are exchangeable. So Choice One is, you are immortalized, but there is no more reproduction on Earth, no pregnancy, no first birthday, no first love'—and I go on and on and on."

Then Barzilai provides an alternative: "Choice Two . . . is you live to be eighty-five and not one day sick, everything healthy and fine, and then one morning you just don't wake up." The response: "Choice One got ten or fifteen people. Everyone else raised their hands for Choice Two."

Over the years, author David Ewing Duncan has polled thirty thousand people about how long they want to live, offering four choices:

- Age 80, approximating current life expectancy
- Age 120, essentially the longest any modern human has lived
- Age 150, close to double the current life span (and, coincidentally, the Prudential pronouncement of the longest-living current person)
- *Forever*, the Silicon Valley darling

According to Duncan, approximately 60 percent choose 80; 30 percent opt for 120; 10 percent select 150. And the forever option? Few takers. Less than 1 percent "embraced the idea that people might avoid death altogether," Duncan says.

LIFE'S GREAT TEACHER

Cheating death is likely to remain both a big business and a headline grabber in the years to come. Too many billionaires simply have it too good to want the music to stop. But at least so far—despite all the dollars spent and hyperbolic pronouncements rendered—there's little evidence that we have to worry about them actually succeeding.

As the *Onion* puts it: "World Death Rate Holding Steady at 100 Percent."

That's a relief. Silicon Valley's plans to conquer death amount to solving the wrong problem, in the wrong way, while creating worse problems in the process.

The right way to conquer death? Well, I think it's safe to say there isn't one. Real happiness and understanding begin, not with denying or defeating death, but with accepting it and living accordingly. The real fountain of youth isn't coming from a "God pill," 150 daily supplements, the well-toned arm of a transfusion associate, Ponce de León's mythical waters in St. Augustine, or hundreds of other misguided and crackpot schemes over the centuries.

The real fountain of youth is in the same place it's always been. It's the fountain *with* youth.

The only true way to endure is to accept our mortality and with it the wisdom that we are a species designed to live on . . . just not literally. We do so by passing on, from generation to generation, what we've learned from life. By investing in and connecting with the next generation, not actually *trying to be* that generation.

That's something that no less a Silicon Valley icon than Steve Jobs understood.

When Jobs gave his now-famous commencement address to the Stanford graduating class of 2005, he argued that death was "the single best invention of life," clearing out the old, making way for the new. Death, said Jobs, having dodged his first brush with pancreatic cancer, is the ultimate reminder of our fundamental condition.

"Remembering that I'll be dead soon is the most important tool I've ever encountered to help me make the big choices in life," Jobs explained. "Because almost everything—all external expectations, all pride, all fear of embarrassment or failure—these things just fall away in the face of death, leaving only what is truly important."

Which leaves us with one question: When all else begins to fall away, what *is* truly important?

BIOLOGY FLOWS DOWNHILL

Mitch Albom's best-selling book *Tuesdays with Morrie* recounts the story of the author's former professor and mentor, Morrie Schwartz, battling ALS in the final months of his life.

"As long as we can love each other, and remember the feeling of love we had, we can die without ever really going away," Schwartz tells him. "All the love you created is still there. All the memories are still there. You live on—in the hearts of everyone you have touched and nurtured while you were here." And in all the hearts of the people they will touch and nurture, he might have added.

Just as Albom is about to turn off his tape recorder to absorb his old teacher's reflections, Schwartz adds another sentence: "Death ends a life, not a relationship."

Schwartz's conviction about the primacy of relationships rings true, especially as we move through midlife and become increasingly aware that there is less time ahead than behind. On a recent morning, as I ate my breakfast, I landed on the obituaries page of the newspaper. The four people profiled had passed away at ages forty-eight, sixty-one, seventy, and eighty-five. I didn't think consciously about it at the time, but for a sixty-year-old, there's a message lurking. The road doesn't go on forever. Our limited time matters more, and so do our relationships.

If someone told you that you had a month left to live, you probably wouldn't start studying Mandarin or the oboe. Most of us would focus on the people we care about, which is precisely what the research of Stanford's Laura Carstensen reveals about our priorities later in life.

Carstensen was initially puzzled when researching older people living in an assisted-living facility. The happiest and best-adjusted residents seemed to be the ones with the fewest social connections. Given what we know about the adverse effects of isolation, especially in later life, Carstensen expected the opposite.

But as she probed deeper, what she found was agency, not isolation. The individuals who were thriving had actively pruned their social ties so that they could concentrate more fully on the people who mattered most. That difficult cousin or the next-door neighbor who complains all the time simply didn't make the list. And that freed up time for the deeper connections, the ones that live on, even beyond our own years—as Mitch Albom's bond with Morrie Schwartz (and for that matter, mine with Gil Stott) did.

Carstensen's insights are captured in her theory of socioemotional selectivity, with its core message that we focus more and more on close relationships as the perceived time ahead grows shorter. This emphasis on the primacy of close ties is further reinforced by numerous additional studies, including the most significant longitudinal research on happiness and well-being in adulthood.

Launched in 1938, the Harvard Study of Adult Development has tracked more than seven hundred men from a wide variety of backgrounds and done so for more than three-quarters of a century. Of the study's findings, one towers above all others: relationships are the critical ingredient in well-being, particularly as we age. In the words of George Vaillant, the Harvard professor who led the study for four decades, "Happiness is love. Full stop."

Robert Waldinger, the study's current director—also a Harvard psychiatry professor and a Zen priest—reports that those who fared best in life were the ones who leaned into close connections not only with family and friends but also with those in the community. This is particularly true in later life. According to Waldinger, close ties help sustain vitality and happiness and forestall decline as we age.

In his book *Aging Well*, Vaillant illuminates the importance not only of bonds with partners and peers but of ties spanning the generations. The Harvard findings show that those in middle age and beyond who invest in caring for and developing the next generation *are three times as likely to be happy* as those who fail to do so.

According to Vaillant, we're wired to connect with those younger than we are and to help create a better future: "The old were put on the earth to nurture the young." It's good for us psychologically and in every other way.

In his exquisite phrasing, "biology flows downhill."

I AM WHAT SURVIVES OF ME

The great pioneer of adult development, Erik Erikson, had a name for all this "flowing downhill." He called it generativity, first defining the idea for the White House Conference on Children and Youth in 1950 as "the concern for establishing and guiding the next generation," which he encapsulated in the phrase "I am what survives of me."

Generativity takes different forms across the life course and can initially be seen in the biological desire to procreate and to parent. But as we move through and beyond midlife, generativity ripens into a broader concern for the next generation, for all the children who will outlive us.

Generativity isn't just about adding life to our later years. It's ultimately about connecting to and nurturing the life that flows *beyond our years*.

Erikson counterposes generativity to stagnation and self-concern, the inability to get past the kind of narcissistic self-obsession behind so much of the immortalists' crusade to conquer death. A truly generative person recognizes that we absorb a great deal from previous generations and are thereby responsible for passing much on to future ones.

It is bittersweet terrain. Life and death, it has been said, are a package deal. Death is heartbreaking, but the idea that important relationships live on eases that sorrow.

For all the bitterness, over the years I've been struck by the joy of generativity. William Blake wrote that "joy and woe are woven fine," and so it is with the generative spirit. The woe is obvious—as anyone who has lost a parent or a spouse or a friend can attest. And there is more and more of that loss as we move into our sixties, seventies, and beyond.

But there is likewise an extraordinary sense of liberation and fulfillment in knowing that one has contributed to life, to the next generation, and to generations after that in ways that will continue to reverberate over time.

LIVING MORTAL

In *Being Mortal,* Atul Gawande explores the connection between mortality and legacy, observing that most people would feel much greater despair about their own mortality if they believed the world was going to end shortly after their own passing. "The only way death is not meaningless is to see yourself as part of something greater," he writes. "If you don't, mortality is only a horror." That "something greater" is the ongoing flow of humanity.

Not long ago, I heard Gawande recount the story of an older woman close to the end. On her deathbed, she told him that the one thing she wanted to do before dying was to take her grandchildren to Disney World, a final generative dream for a shared experience that the children would always have to remember her by. She died two days after talking to Gawande.

"We had missed that," Gawande said. "We had failed. We had never asked her." If the doctors had bothered to really listen to her, they would have made different medical decisions. If they had known a month earlier what really mattered to her, she could have taken that trip.

After listening to Gawande, I came away convinced that we all need to do a better job of asking about and listening to the final wishes of those who are dying.

But likewise, I wondered, why do we wait so long to embrace what mortality has to teach us? Can't we do better than waiting until our final months and weeks and days to suggest the things we hope to be remembered by? To make those commitments and take those actions that will live on beyond our days?

I think we can do better, thanks to a great opportunity taking shape today, an opportunity that earlier generations all too rarely had—one that exists at the intersection of longevity and mortality, of extending life while accepting death.

Almost a century ago, G. Stanley Hall, the father of American psychology and the person who put adolescence on the map, argued that the life course was changing in profound ways. A new period was opening up between the middle years and true old age. He termed this period an "Indian summer."

Human beings, in Hall's words, didn't reach the height of their capacities until the "shadows begin to slant eastward, and for a season, which varies greatly with individuals, our powers increase as the shadows lengthen."

The way I figure it, the shadows slanting eastward amount to the perfect intersection of time lived, time left to live, and our connection to the time beyond our lives. It's that season when we know what matters and have the time and capacity—and the motivation—to do something significant with it.

Today, we're witnessing a population explosion of individuals flooding into that Indian summer, truly one of the sweet spots in life. Recently the *Wall Street Journal* asked if there is a perfect age, generating a multiplicity of choices. To me, this is that perfect age.

Some have described this time as an oxymoronic period, a time of confusion and contradiction, but I believe it has the potential to be the season of generativity, the chance to make some of our most important and resonant contributions to future generations.

A period when we can do more than "be mortal." We can actually live mortal.

THE WORLD IS CALLING

In *The Last Word*, a 2017 film, Shirley MacLaine plays an unlikable, controlling yet successful former businesswoman. Age and loneliness prompt her to obsess about mortality and the things others will say about her when she's gone. In an effort to control her legacy, she first tries strong-arming the local newspaper's obituary writer to embellish the story of her life and good deeds. It doesn't work. Nobody the obituary writer talks to—her former spouse, daughter, business associates, neighbors—has anything good to say about MacLaine's character.

Undeterred, she next tries to rewrite her legacy by superficially changing her life. The ensuing story involves her—cynically at first, more genuinely as events unfold—befriending both the twenty-something obituary writer and a spirited and irascible young African American girl at the school where she makes a sizeable philanthropic gift. Shockingly (I know you are shocked), MacLaine's character is transformed by the relationships and by living the life she wants to be remembered for—indeed, by living mortal.

The story is a parable of what *New York Times* columnist David Brooks calls the "eulogy virtues," contrasting them with the "résumé virtues" that consume much of our lives. For Brooks, eulogy virtues are the ones we want to be remembered for at our memorial services (beyond, "Look, he's moving!"). They are about character and love, relationships and commitments, generativity and legacy. As *The Last Word* depicts, longer lives offer the possibility of a second chance at influencing our legacy, and perhaps even a shot at redemption.

MacLaine is hardly the only celebrity to play out a version of this story on the movie screen. In recent years Bill Murray, Maggie Smith,

Laurence Fishburne, Clint Eastwood, Judi Dench, Robert De Niro, and various others have taken their turn. More than just a parade of actors reaching their Indian summer (and doing a few small movies here and there), this story plays out in some of the biggest, most revered characters in movie-franchise history, from Luke Skywalker to Rocky.

In *Creed*, the seventh movie in the series, Sylvester Stallone plays a weather-beaten sixty-something Rocky—past his glory and largely alone. His beloved wife, Adrian, has died of ovarian cancer. He's returned to his roots, sleepwalking through life's remaining years at his South Philadelphia restaurant. His most significant accomplishments, what he'll be remembered for, seem long behind him.

This all changes when a young fighter named Donny, the son of Rocky's former rival and departed friend, Apollo Creed, enters his life. Donny's father died before he was born, but the young man feels compelled to learn more about him and follow his own destiny as a fighter. Having ditched his corporate career in Los Angeles for a shot in the ring, Donny moves to Philadelphia to persuade Rocky to train him.

Of course, Rocky wants no part of it, having closed the chapter on boxing. Ultimately, he relents (or there would be no movie). As the two start working together, Rocky becomes both a link for the young fighter to the parent he never knew and a kind of surrogate father. Donny calls him "Unc," for uncle. It's a tale of extended kinship, one that crosses race, age, and blood (lots of blood).

The mentoring relationship gives Rocky a purpose in life—and redemption. Still, when he's diagnosed with lymphoma, his instinct is to accept that fate. After all, cancer treatments did little to save Adrian. The young fighter convinces Rocky to take on the disease, not for himself but because Donny needs him.

What strikes me when watching the film is how much more nuanced and layered it is than the earlier blockbuster iterations of the Rocky character. *Creed* is a story of generativity, but it's also one driven by a younger person, dislodging an older one from a kind of withdrawal while demanding wisdom and care, traits the older character believes the world no longer wants or needs.

The *Creed* story line recurs in a string of other films in recent years, including *The Last Jedi*, in which the young warrior Rey seeks out an aging Luke Skywalker, who has retreated into seclusion—a self-imposed ice floe—and implores him to train her in the ancient ways.

In these roles, the older characters not only find purpose in later life but uncover deeper needs; in finding redemption and rejuvenation, these elders discover the fountain *with* youth.

They realize that they are genuinely needed by a younger generation navigating the path to, and through, adulthood with too little support.

True on the big screen and in real life, as I discovered for myself some thirty years ago.

Chapter 2

LOVE AND DEATH

In 1955, a twenty-six-year-old psychologist named Emmy Werner launched a study of all 698 children born that year on the Hawaiian island of Kauai. That longitudinal research would last for forty years and become, like the Harvard Study of Adult Development, a landmark in our understanding of how humans thrive.

Sounds like a plum assignment, visiting Kauai for forty years. But the island Werner encountered in 1955 was a place of grinding poverty, high levels of alcohol abuse and mental illness, and widespread family dysfunction for residents eking out a harsh living working on the island's sugar plantations.

Werner predicted that these risk factors would weigh heavily on the children in her research, and she was right. Many of the young people she studied ended up struggling in life. But that wasn't the main news. Werner's great breakthrough came through understanding those who managed to "overcome the odds," to paraphrase the title of one of Werner's books, the children who proved "vulnerable yet invincible."

Up until that point, most psychologists and other experts determined to understand the problems facing young people who had been termed "juvenile delinquents" examined children who had failed. They hoped to understand what went wrong and uncover ways to turn those challenges around. Werner had a different idea.

Why not study the young people who made it despite having so much thrown at them? What if we tried to understand the "protective factors" that buffered children—along with the risk factors that compromised their lives—and tried to reproduce those positive factors for more young people? Beginning in the 1970s, Werner began calling these successful children resilient.

As Werner predicted, a subgroup of the children of Kauai turned out to be just that. Despite an array of adverse circumstances—alcoholic or mentally ill parents, family breakup and dysfunction, unemployment, and material deprivation—they turned into "caring, competent and confident" adults.

What did these resilient children have in common?

Werner found that one factor stood out in particular: the presence of a caring adult beyond the immediate family—a mentor, an aunt, a coach, a teacher, a neighbor who took the younger person under his or her wing. Involvement in a community group like a church or the Y also proved to be an important buffer, as did a set of internal beliefs and attitudes that helped protect the individual from the full corrosive force of their circumstances.

THE BIG QUESTION

By the time I met Emmy Werner, she was already in her sixties, living in Berkeley and teaching at the University of California, Davis. One of the first tenured women faculty members at Davis, Werner progressed from studying the children of Kauai to, more broadly, examining the experience of children growing up in an array of war-torn and stressful circumstances.

I had recently moved to Berkeley myself and was in the midst of writing my first book, *The Kindness of Strangers*, on the promise and pitfalls of mentoring for young people. At the time, I was working for a nonprofit organization created by the Ford Foundation, dedicated to developing new ways to help young people who were growing up against the odds, the same kinds of kids who were the subject of Werner's research.

I started working for the group at twenty-six, the age Emmy was when she began her research in Kauai. A newly minted Yale MBA, I'd decided against heading into management consulting (a full quarter of my class went to McKinsey) or investment banking (having barely survived the one required finance class in my MBA program). Instead, I was drawn to do something to fight poverty at a time when inequality and division in America were becoming increasingly pronounced.

But not long into my new job, I was already uncomfortable with the prevailing wisdom of the field. The technocratic social scientists who predominated in education and social policy at that time had concocted complicated and bloodless approaches to place young people on a path to success. As far as I could tell, these models were primarily well suited for one thing: being measured by the mathematical tools the specialists had at their disposal.

In particular, there was skepticism about anything that depended on the role of human beings. The "experts" viewed the personal element in schools and youth organizations as an unpredictable input that made reliable evaluation elusive. If it wasn't measurable, they seemed to be saying, it couldn't possibly be meaningful. These were the days when some extolled "teacher-proof curricula," aimed at creating schools insulated from the irascibility of actual people, such as teachers.

What did the kids think of all this? When my colleagues and I bothered to talk with them about their experience, these young people showed little interest in the experts' complex concoctions. They often tried to change the subject, and they almost always said the same thing: what mattered most were people who cared. Sometimes a teacher, sometimes a counselor or a coach or a grandparent figure. They needed a person who showed an interest in them, who listened, who took the time to forge a connection.

Discovering Werner's research and the broader resilience field was like coming in from the cold. For me, the Kauai longitudinal study echoed and underscored what the young people I met said was essential. It was what I had experienced through my own relationship with Gil Stott, that caring and connection were of essential importance.

Full stop. As the eminent Cornell professor and child psychologist Urie Bronfenbrenner would famously concluded, "Every child needs at least one adult who is irrationally crazy about him or her."

After moving to Berkeley, I decided to reach out to Werner to learn more about her work and maybe get a little moral support in the process. To my surprise, she responded. And to my delight, over the coming years we became good friends.

A tiny, round woman no more than five feet tall with a thick German accent and a high-pitched, quavering voice, Emmy had a habit of closing her eyes when she was about to make an important point. Knowing her was a little like having my own personal faculty adviser, a trusted mentor, and a surrogate grandmother all rolled into one.

Emmy was at once intellectually demanding and irrationally crazy about her students. It was a winning combination. And it came from the heart. Her decision to study children growing up under harsh circumstances was hardly a coincidence. She had grown up in Germany during World War II, in the Rhine city of Eltville, surviving years of bombing raids as a child. Her father was the only male in his family to survive the war. Even into her eighties, she instinctively leapt forward and covered her head when a car backfired or a siren sounded.

We hung out in the hipster cafés of Berkeley, making an odd couple, both of us out of place. I was without a nearby family of my own, living on the other side of the country from where I'd grown up. Emmy and her husband, Stan Jacobsen, a retired psychologist and former military man, became an extended West Coast family. I often went to dinner at their house or joined them at the club they frequented for naval officers on Treasure Island in San Francisco Bay.

Emmy helped me with my book, pressing me on one question in particular, which I knew was an important one because she closed her eyes when asking it. Yes, powerful bonds with caring adults—often unrelated adults, often older people—made all the difference for the resilient children of Kauai and elsewhere. But those children also showed a remarkable ability to recruit these adults themselves. They seemed to possess, inherently, the skills required to forge relationships with caring adults.

Would connecting caring adults with young people who didn't already have the internal wherewithal to find them on their own produce similar benefits? I pressed back, asking Emmy what she thought. She closed her eyes, paused briefly, and told me that she didn't know definitively, but she suspected they would. We both believed that it was possible to create these kinds of bonds beyond family and beyond those children who already contained abundant gifts of resilience.

I set out to prove it.

Along the way, I started an organization, created programs, wrote more books, and had a family of my own. Life got increasingly frenzied. And, sadly, I lost touch with Emmy, even though we ended up living just a mile apart. Periodically, I would vow to get back in touch, but I invariably ended up distracted by the next deadline or item on the to-do list.

This past October I found myself thinking about Emmy and all the gratitude and affection I had for her. I searched for her email address in my inbox, to no avail. I then located her faculty page at the University of California, Davis, which listed Werner as emeritus and featured a 2015 video of Emmy reflecting on resilience and her work over more than half a century. She was still exuding kindness while saying dazzling things.

I wrote her with regrets for having waited so long to be back in touch. I provided updates on developments personal and professional, offered warm wishes to her and Stan, and asked if they'd like to get together.

Within an hour, there was a note back from Stan. Emmy had died the previous week, at age eighty-eight.

"I am heartbroken," he wrote.

WHERE ARE THE HUMANS?

It took a few years, but we got an answer to Emmy's big question, wrapped in a study of the Big Brothers Big Sisters program.

In the 1980s, new mentoring programs were popping up around the country, touting their benefits. These programs were run at a fraction of the cost of the much older Big Brothers Big Sisters, prompting the venerable program to want to prove its effectiveness (and justify its expense). They asked the nonprofit research organization I was working for, Public/Private Ventures, to conduct a study on the importance of caring-adult relationships for children and youth coming from vulnerable backgrounds.

Big Brothers Big Sisters served primarily children from single-parent, low-income families. While seventy thousand children in the United States were being matched with "bigs" at the time, thirty thousand more were languishing on the waiting list for an average of eighteen months. The backlog was undeniably bad for children but constituted a gold mine for social-science researchers.

Our team was able to take one thousand kids on the waiting list and randomly assign mentors to half. The other half were promised "bigs" at the end of the eighteen months, the period they would have waited anyway. But first, during that year and a half, the Public/Private Ventures' researchers compared young people who had mentors with the young people who didn't have them.

The contrast was staggering. There was a 46 percent difference in drug use, a 50 percent difference in school truancy, and a 33 percent difference in violent behavior. These numbers so far outstripped even the most heralded programs focused on combating these problems that we came to the only logical conclusion: there must have been a methodological error. We hauled in a bevy of academic experts, but they came up empty.

We were left with an inescapable conclusion: relationships matter, just as they had with the resilient children in Kauai and in other studies of young people who found these bonds in the "natural" world. And our research showed that relationships could in fact be fostered, to great benefit.

We even learned lessons about how. The critical ingredient was time. These mentors spent ten to twelve hours a month with young people. These were consistent connections requiring serious commitment. We likewise learned that mentors couldn't rush these connections. Those who swooped in with a strategic plan for transforming the life of the child in efficient fashion were dismal failures. After nine months, only a handful of these "bigs" and "littles" were still meeting.

But mentors who took their time, played catch, and went to McDonald's were having a massive impact on the lives of these young people. It turns out that forging these caring-adult connections is a little like baking a soufflé. Rush, and it collapses; provide patience and care, and something significant rises.

This lesson was brought home to me through the story of a mentor—a Big Brother in Oakland in my memory—who came to understand the importance of developing a true partnership with a young person, one in which the child takes equal responsibility for cultivating and building the bond.

After several months of meetings between the two, this mentor told his Little Brother that the boy could name the activity the two would do together next time they met. It would be up to him, within reason. A week later, the mentor arrived and asked the youngster what they should do that afternoon. The Little Brother demurred. After almost an hour of trying to coax the boy to express what he wanted, the disappointed mentor said he needed to go home. They could pick up where they left off the following week.

At that point, the boy anxiously asked the mentor to stay, finally revealing what he wanted. Not to go bowling or eat hamburgers or play catch. He wanted to see the man shave. He'd never seen a man shave before and was beginning to grow his first facial hair.

As this story illustrates, the Big Brothers Big Sisters research may have underplayed one of the most important outcomes of all—the intrinsic value of passing our fundamental humanity from generation to generation. Yet, for all the encouragement of the study's results, the special bonds between "bigs" and "littles," and the many stories like this one, there was still an uncomfortable elephant lingering in the room.

If all this worked so well, why were thirty thousand children stuck month after month on the waiting list? Where were the people to mentor them, the human beings to do those things that only people can do? There simply weren't enough in the group primarily targeted for recruitment by Big Brothers Big Sisters at the time—adults in their twenties, thirties, and forties who barely had enough time for their own children (and jobs), much less ten to twelve hours a month for someone else's child.

This question—*Where are the humans to do those things only humans can do?*—led me to think more broadly about people who had time. Already the media and researchers alike were sounding alarms about the doubling of the over-sixty population just around the corner. This was where the demographics were heading, where so much human capital was accumulating.

And time studies showed that this group had a near monopoly on discretionary time. How were they spending it? Mostly watching TV. (And not even good TV—this was long before Amazon and Netflix and the renaissance on the little screen.) What's more, and not surprising in the context of all the TV viewing, research was emerging about the "purpose gap" facing so many over sixty.

Could "olders" join the "bigs" to help "littles"? It seemed like a win-win in the making—good for kids, good for older people, good for the social fabric. But would it actually work? And where were the places where this activity was already underway?

DON'T BE LIKE ME

My journey of discovery began with a program I'd heard about from a colleague, the Work Connection, in Saugus, Massachusetts, a town on the North Shore near Boston. The son of an innovative union leader named Peter DeCicco had run into problems with the law for nonviolent property crime. The teenager was brought before a judge and forced to pay a fine—which meant that DeCicco paid the fine because his son didn't have a job. It didn't make sense to the father, who wished there had been an option for his son to pay restitution to the victim of his crime. A few conversations later, DeCicco realized it didn't make sense to the judge either.

Together, DeCicco and several judges created the Work Connection to enable young people who had committed nonviolent crimes to make things right by paying victims for their loss, avoiding conventional fines and even jail time.

Great idea, with one major hitch. How would the young people get work so they could earn the money to make restitution payments? DeCicco had an answer. Retired union members who primarily worked at the nearby Lynn, Massachusetts, General Electric plant had taken to hanging out every day at the International Union of Electrical Workers' union office, DeCicco's workplace. They were bored silly.

It dawned on DeCicco that these retirees had the necessary experience and connections to help the young people in the restitution program find work. And he was right. I remember my visit vividly, first spending time in a conference room with the retiree-mentors, who had been matched with struggling young people. The retirees were sitting around a table, comparing notes on their "cases." If I didn't know better, I would have thought I'd walked into a group of social workers doing their thing. In fact, the (mostly) men around the table were retired electrical workers, police officers, and firefighters. Also in the room: George Reilly, the former head of the local Teamsters Union, who was known for practicing tough love, emphasis on the "tough."

Another day I went out with one of the mentors and his charge and saw the wisdom of experience in action. The union retiree took the young person to the local diner where contractors went for breakfast before heading out to their daily jobs. The retiree knew he would run into guys at the diner he'd known over the years, giving him an excuse to introduce them to his charge. Next thing you know, the youth had a job assisting at a construction site—and a foot in the door of the working world.

There is a theory in sociology known as the "strength of weak ties," which, applied here, argues that working-class youth get jobs not through their close relatives or friends but through more extended networks that can be powerful. It may not work every time, but I witnessed the strength of weak ties in action in Saugus and in the Work Connection.

At the same time, the mentors were the antithesis of conventional role models. Rather than trying to get young people to emulate them or take their advice, the Work Connection mentors instead talked candidly about their missteps and mistakes. And there were plenty.

Nick Spaneas, a particularly compelling mentor who'd had his own ups and downs in life, essentially counseled his "kid" *to not be like him*, to avoid the stupid mistakes he'd made that had caused him, and others, a lot of pain. Paired with a young man who had been living outside in a refrigerator box, Nick didn't want to see the youth go down the same troubled road he'd traveled. Nick's efforts to help the boy seemed, in some measure, a way toward redemption— and a pragmatic one at that.

EVERY DOLLAR SPENT TWICE

The Work Connection was a stop on the road to my primary destination, the Teen Moms program run by Foster Grandparents in Portland, Maine.

Foster Grandparents was created nationally in 1965 as part of the War on Poverty. Its simple model pairs unrelated older people with young people who are either developmentally disabled or economically disadvantaged. The program wasn't created out of a vision for the potential of intergenerational bonds but rather out of Lyndon Johnson's determination to fight poverty among the elderly.

In the early 1960s, before Medicare was enacted and Social Security spread to a wider swath of the population, between a third and half of seniors were living below the poverty line. In spite of the scale of the problem, Johnson ran into congressional opposition to giving more financial support to seniors. So the administration got creative. Foster Grandparents was, to some extent, a ruse to get around this congressional barrier. By creating a program and offering the equivalent of the minimum wage to impoverished seniors—mostly women—the federal government could put desperately needed dollars into their pockets.

There was little hope that the role itself would be much more than make-work. That view was shared by social service agencies around the country, which for the most part were strong-armed into submitting proposals to operate Foster Grandparents programs. These agencies' indifference (at best) and resistance (often) was so strong that federal employees working for Sargent Shriver's Office of Economic Opportunity were dispatched to visit local agencies around the country and actually write the proposals for them. In effect, they wrote the proposals and submitted them to . . . themselves. Miraculously, the applications were then approved and funded.

Soon after the program was implemented, it became clear that there was a simple genius to both the model and its name. Foster Grandparents matched unrelated older people who had life experience and a need to be needed with young people craving individualized support, in ways that approximated aspects of the grandparent relationship. Today Foster Grandparents involves about twenty-five thousand low-income individuals over sixty spending fifteen to forty hours a week with high-needs children and youth throughout the United States. The program's informal motto—"Every dollar spent twice"—gets at the vast mutual benefit involved, a smart approach for our fiscally challenged times.

Indeed, when I visited Sargent Shriver in the late 1990s to talk with him about the War on Poverty, he described Foster Grandparents as one of the initiative's proudest achievements. Then he pulled out a black ashtray with the names and insignias of all the War on Poverty programs stenciled around the outside. Foster Grandparents, Head Start, Volunteers in Service to America (VISTA), and more. Thinking back, I can't help but chuckle. The components of the War on Poverty, an initiative with a strong emphasis on promoting health, were memorialized on an ashtray.

When I asked Shriver to say more about his enthusiasm for Foster Grandparents, so many years after its creation, he responded without hesitation: "It worked! And it worked for two reasons. First of all, it's human—it's about human relationships. Second, it's simple. It was one of those simple ideas that, I think, are frequently the best ideas."

Patsy LaViolette was one of the first Foster Grandparents I met in Portland. Her role: to help teenage mothers navigate their way through lonely waters. Each day, Monday through Thursday, she drove to a teen mom's home and spent five hours visiting. Like many of the union retirees I'd met in Saugus, Patsy was a survivor, having raised three children alone after her husband died, working as a cashier, bookkeeper, nurse's aide, and beautician. Patsy had stores of life experience as a parent. Although she wasn't particularly close with her own daughter, she was able to forge close ties with the young mothers she worked with. There was no family baggage there.

I also spent time with John Curtis, a navy veteran and retired employee of W. T. Grant, and one of the few men enrolled in Foster Grandparents in Portland. With his goatee and laid-back manner, John reminded me of Pete Seeger. Years before, he had nearly died from heart disease, and I got a strong sense that Curtis had come face to face with existential questions and that those encounters had left him determined to live out whatever time he had in a way that made a better life for others.

"I feel I owe my community," he said. "I have to pay back, be thankful for my life, and maybe this is one way of doing it. The other thing is my own grandchildren are a hundred miles away from me, and I can't see them as much. And I would hope that somebody where they live had interest in them, too. . . . I think they need somebody with a little experience, who really cares. And it just helps me to know that I am needed somewhere."

AGGIE AND LOUISE

Aggie Bennett and Louise Casey were known as sisters by the staff and children on the pediatrics ward of Maine Medical Center, where they'd spent over a decade working as Foster Grandparents. Aggie was "the tall one," at four feet eleven, while Louise didn't quite measure up at four feet ten and a half.

They'd worked hard all their lives, Aggie as a waitress and Louise in a sawmill. Rather than experiencing retirement as a well-deserved rest in their early sixties, neither felt comfortable sitting around. Aggie told me she didn't "want to rust away"; she "wanted to wear away" doing something more useful than sitting in a chair making silk coat hangers at the local senior center. Louise became a lay minister in her church.

Their personalities were dramatically different. Aggie was brash, the center of attention. Louise demure, soothing, and kindly. One of my first encounters with Aggie was watching her, dressed as a tiger, chase children around the pediatrics ward as part of a costume parade. When I asked her whether she still enjoyed doing this work after so many years, she told me, "It's not a job—it's a joy."

Year after year, day after day, twenty hours each week, even during harsh Maine winters, Aggie and Louise made their way to Maine Medical Center, a beautiful set of nineteenth-century and modern buildings on the city's dramatic western promenade. I spent over a year making periodic visits to them, staying in the quirky Pomegranate Inn, in the adjacent neighborhood filled with gracious Victorian homes. All the walls in the inn were painted by local artists.

I loved waking up in what seemed like a painting, walking through a tree-lined neighborhood, and visiting Aggie and Louise, who (most especially Louise) became an important part of my life. When I'd visit, Aggie, Louise, and I would go out to dinner by the wharf for early-bird specials. For years, until she passed away, Louise would send me Hall-mark cards with big, grandmotherly handwriting on my birthday.

Created in 1864, Maine Medical Center, then, as it is today, was the finest and the biggest hospital in Maine. The pediatrics ward featured state-of-the-art technology and highly trained doctors and nurses. It was the place where children battling serious illnesses in the region went for treatment. In a big state stretching up to the Canadian border, that often meant parents traveling hours from home.

Maine is also a poor state. Many parents of sick children there couldn't afford to leave jobs indefinitely to remain at their children's side. They were frequently forced to return home, hundreds of miles away, to their other children and to jobs in sawmills and as waitresses and in other modestly paying roles that they could ill afford to leave.

That's where Aggie and Louise came in. The women were fixtures on the pediatrics ward in much the way that Gil Stott had been a fixture at Swarthmore College. Like Gil, they had formal roles that didn't capture their true value. And that value extended beyond tiger costumes.

Imagine being eight years old, facing cancer or another terrifying illness, maybe being in pain, hundreds of miles from home, in an institutional setting, without your parents. Aggie and Louise filled that breach. They sat with the kids, entertaining them, explaining things to them, comforting them. They became family to these children, and the kids became family to them. It was a joy and a source of deep meaning and purpose.

Yet "joy and woe are woven fine," most especially on the pediatrics ward.

It was the woe that was on my mind when I asked Aggie and Louise whether they ever considered quitting, aware as anyone would be of the suffering and tragedy built into the nature of a hospital caring for extremely ill children. At some point, I asked, "Did it simply become too hard to be in the presence of that kind of sadness?"

Aggie was uncharacteristically quiet when I asked her this question, Louise at her side. I thought that perhaps they were angry with me for voicing something difficult that they didn't want to talk about. But what ensued became an indelible exchange for me—one that's stayed with me for over thirty years.

Louise began, reflectively: "Everybody will say, 'How can you take it when you lose a child?' and I think Aggie and I feel the same way— heartbroken. . . . But if we can do something when they're here to make that little child happy, to smile, it's worth it all. We lose them, and it is heartbreaking."

"I don't think I'd been here a year," Aggie continued, "when Sue Forth was head of the unit, and she asked me, 'How strong a person are you?' I said, 'Well, I've always prided myself that I was strong.' She says, 'We got a baby that is dying, and we promised that mother that her baby would not die in a crib. Do you think you could hold her?' Well, they put me in a room here, they kept checking on me, and that baby didn't die in no crib . . . that baby died in my arms. And I was always so grateful for that. I didn't feel fear . . . I just felt good. You know how it is, Louise, when you just sit with them, and your heart's aching, but you don't let them know it, that's all."

Louise was nodding her head, sobbing quietly. "They let me go in and sit with Tanya after she died. They said, 'Would you feel better?' because I loved her so. And they said, 'Would you feel better just going in and sitting for a while?' And I said, 'Yes I would.' And Cheryl, I was there when Cheryl died, almost in my arms . . ."

"You know something, though," Aggie continued. "It does make you a stronger person. It does."

Spending time with Aggie and Louise made *me* a stronger person, a wiser one, and though they've been gone for so many years now, it's not hard for me to conjure them up. They taught me much about purpose in later life, about love across the generations.

One of those lessons was blindingly simple. "We don't have a single person to waste," observed Maggie Kuhn, who founded the Gray Panthers in the 1970s to fight ageism and bring the generations together. No one who visited the pediatrics ward of Maine Medical Center could leave feeling that it was okay to create a society where older people like Aggie and Louise sat in isolated apartments watching TV while children were left abandoned in hospital wards a mile away.

I went to Portland wondering how we could allocate human assets to meet human needs, asking, "Where are the human beings to do those things only humans can do?" I left with little question about the answer—and with a life's calling laid out in front of me. I would try to help create in the world more of what I had witnessed while visiting Aggie and Louise.

I had absorbed what Emmy Werner, Urie Bronfenbrenner, and other scholars had to teach about the power of a caring adult in a young person's life. I had seen directly how much younger people, myself included, needed what older people could deliver. And I was determined to put the two big puzzle pieces—older adults' need to nurture and young people's need to be nurtured—together.

Looking back, I see now that I was also witnessing a deeper story, one that extended beyond matching supply and demand. In the few minutes it took for a young boy to see an older man shave for the first time or for a child to spend her final moments in the arms of an old woman, something crossed from one generation to the next, from one person to the next. Some might call it instinctual or fundamentally human or even tragic. I can only call it love.

At the time, I didn't fully grasp all of that. My mind was flooded with the questions right in front of me. If we don't have a single person to waste, I wondered, why do we continue to write off so many of the most experienced people in society? Why wasn't what I'd witnessed in Saugus and Portland happening everywhere? How is it that we'd managed, so thoroughly, to lose our way?

Chapter 3

AGE APARTHEID

It all started with Big Ben Schleifer.

The transformation of later life in America in the middle of the twentieth century. The rebranding of retirement as an attempt to recapture one's youth. The dream of graying as playing. The rise of age-segregated, seniors-only sunshine cities that would come to embody the new norm for the golden years. The cultural ideals and institutional arrangements that have come to stymie ties between the generations and seed many of the challenges we face today.

And it all began with the best of intentions.

Benjamin "Big Ben" Schleifer was born in 1901 outside Minsk, in what is now Belarus. In 1914, his family came to New York, desperate to escape anti-Semitism and the terror of Cossack raids. An inveterate reader who would scour the subway for abandoned newspapers, Schleifer was nevertheless forced to quit school in his early teens to help support his family, holding down one manual job after another to make ends meet.

Schleifer's youthful milieu was also the socialism of Depression-era immigrant New York, defined by groups like the Workmen's Circles. The young man's experiences at the time helped shape his humanitarian instincts and concern for those less fortunate. He was also a restless innovator with a feel for business and entrepreneurship.

In 1947, Schleifer's asthma prompted him to move to Phoenix in hopes of finding a cure, or at least some relief from the condition. The postwar Phoenix that Schleifer encountered was hardly the sprawling metropolis of today. And it was a far cry from the New York that Schleifer had left behind.

Phoenix was essentially in the middle of nowhere, surrounded by miles of cotton fields and ranches, a beautiful but sleepy hamlet. But more and more people like Schleifer had started to move there for its warm temperatures and salubrious desert climate. Development was picking up, and Schleifer saw an opportunity in the city's growing housing industry. He put his stake in the ground, starting Big Ben Realty.

Schleifer still traveled home to New York whenever he could, and on one such trip, he went to see an elderly friend living in a Rochester, New York, nursing home. The confined, lifeless existence his friend endured there roused his compassion, indignation, and entrepreneurial instincts. Who would want to end up in one of those places? He felt there had to be another way—perhaps some type of communal living, like a kibbutz. He thought of a Jewish prayer he used to hear when he was a child in Minsk: "Do not forsake me, God, when I get old."

Back in Arizona, Schleifer began developing plans for a new community, exclusively for older people of modest means, that would be the diametric opposite of the nursing home existence he encountered in Rochester. It would offer a sense of connection and acceptance— an antidote to the loneliness, boredom, rejection, and inactivity that characterized his friend's final years. According to Andrew Blechman, author of *Leisureville*, Schleifer determined to name this new development Youngtown to ensure that it "would be associated with youth and ambition," helping "to make elderly people not feel old."

In 1954, Schleifer forged a partnership to develop a 320-acre dairy and cattle ranch near Peoria, Arizona, twenty miles outside Phoenix. As he put his plan into action, affordability became a central goal. He knew what it was like to be strapped for cash.

During his own move to Phoenix, Schleifer had spent time living in his car, too poor to pay his rent. On several occasions, he was bailed out by the kindness of strangers. A benevolent landlord let him stay in an apartment for months rent-free. In another case, a local developer stuffed forty dollars in Schleifer's pocket, asking nothing in return. A proud and ethical man, Schleifer paid them both back, promising the developer to do so with great dividends (which he did, writing the developer into future deals reportedly returning thousands of dollars).

The decision to create Youngtown as the first community of its type exclusively for older people was not made out of antipathy for children. By all accounts Schleifer loved kids and was good with them. But Schleifer knew that children brought costs, like taxes to pay for schools, and his top priority was to ensure that senior citizens subsisting on Social Security could afford to live at Youngtown.

By 1955, 125 houses were completed, 85 of them selling quickly. On a sweltering July day in 2017 when I visited the tiny log cabin that today constitutes the Youngtown Historical Society, I was surrounded by photos and floor plans for the original models, bare-bones dwellings with grandiose names that invoked their desert surroundings. Anybody for the Saguaro, or the Cholla, or the Yucca? How about the Ocotillo? In the grainy marketing photographs of the day, it's hard to discern much difference between the models.

Schleifer's seat-of-the-pants marketing skills proved well tuned to selling this fountain of youth in the middle of the desert. Youngtown's promise of a supportive community and inexpensive living for older people was an appealing alternative in a country increasingly hostile to the elderly. Many were captivated by the dream of finding their own second youth, apart from the clamor and costs of children.

The turning point for Schleifer's project was a November 24, 1957, special about Youngtown on Dave Garroway's national NBC television show, *Wide, Wide World,* boasting four million viewers across the country. Entitled "Miracle in the Desert," Garroway's show described Youngtown as "a community dedicated to the belief that retirement need not mean the end of fruitful activity or the loss of personal dignity. The townspeople, all over fifty years of age, have come from every part of the country to live in the Southwest's sunshine and enjoy its way of life."

Youngtown's opening coincided with a national infatuation not just with leisure but with the American teenager. Weeks earlier, in a segment entitled, "In Between," Garroway featured the "unpredictable, fun-filled and sometimes controversial segment of America—the teenagers." Youngtown promised to bring some of that magic to the supposedly over-the-hill set.

It worked. The community would not only capture the nation's imagination; it would become home to the very first AARP chapter in America.

But not all was sun drenched and rosy. Although Schleifer promoted the idea of an affordable, age-segregated Youngtown, somehow he was still surprised and unhappy when the town's residents banded together to vote down a local school bond issue that would have raised taxes.

In any case, the restless entrepreneur was ready to move on. More captivated by starting something new than by taking Youngtown to scale, he decided that his next project would be even closer to his ideals and experience—a Jewish version of the Youngtown model. Why not create a kibbutz for working-class Jewish retirees? Venturing twenty miles deeper into the desert, Schleifer launched Circle City, named partly to honor the Workmen's Circles of his youth but also to reflect streets organized in circular patterns to promote neighborliness.

Sadly, few showed up—and the project's collapse ruined him financially.

According to author Andrew Blechman, Schleifer spent his remaining years getting by on Social Security, playing cards with friends in a Phoenix park, and, by all reports, living out a happy retirement, if not an affluent one. In many ways, it was the kind of retirement he had hoped to make more widely available through Youngtown and Circle City both.

But the Youngtown idea didn't end there. The original community itself continued to evolve and grow steadily. And then developer Del Webb embraced Big Ben Schleifer's model. Webb's Sun City, patterned after Youngtown and located directly across the street from it, became the prototype for vast seniors-only, golf-and-leisure towns that soon spread throughout the country and powered a multibillion-dollar housing industry, in the process redefining what it meant to grow older in America.

TOO OLD TO WORK, TOO YOUNG TO DIE

When the Puritans arrived in Massachusetts in 1629, they would have seen little need for a refuge for old people, much less one in the middle of the desert, cut off from the rest of humanity and dedicated to the ideal of youthfulness. They had no desire to live long or to feel younger. They weren't trying to find the fountain of youth. If anything, they'd have chosen its opposite. Those early Americans lived short lives, revered age, and sought to get old as quickly as possible. Indeed, historians have termed the Puritan colonies a gerontocracy.

According to the popular watchword of the era, "A hoary head"—white haired—"is a crown of gold." Becoming old in the seventeenth century was a relative rarity—median age at the time hovered around sixteen—but it was also considered a sign from the divine, an indication that one had lived a life full of grace. In fact, so covetous were the Puritans of reaching a ripe old age that they tried to fake it.

They lied on the census to say they were two or three years older than they actually were (we, of course, do just the opposite). The Puritan colony featured specially trained tailors adept at making their clients look slumped over. They wore hoary-headed wigs. In keeping, the Puritans' image of Jesus was not the youthful figure seen so often today but rather a sage-like septuagenarian with locks "white like wool."

At a time of limited literacy, elders were counted on to be "keepers of the culture," according to historian David Hackett Fischer, "living representatives of the past, armed with ancient precedents and cloaked in the authority of ancestral ways." Deference was paid to the experience of the oldest inhabitant and to the judgment of "ancient men" and "reverent women." The iconography of the period is filled with images of older people supporting and engaging with children.

But by the nineteenth century, age as status began to unravel. Older people grew a little too enamored of their crown of gold and somewhat haughty about their revered position, producing a backlash from younger generations. Still the senior set remained in the mainstream through the 1800s, and the largely agrarian country was thoroughly integrated by age. Multiple generations lived under the same roof, toiled side by side in the fields, and worshipped together in congregations. Even education in one-room schoolhouses brought students of different ages together—some in their twenties and thirties.

Overall, there was little awareness of numerical age in American society. Birthdays weren't celebrated; indeed, most individuals would have been hard pressed to name their own birthday. In nineteenth-century America, few noticed or would even think to ask.

That all changed in the twentieth century.

How did we get from a state of obliviousness about age to today's profoundly age-conscious America, where birthdays—especially milestone birthdays—are a big deal, newspaper articles scrupulously list individuals' ages, and public policy entitlements are commonly linked to age? How exactly did we shift from a society that revered older people to one that came to denigrate them? How did hanging on to one's fading youth become a frenzied pursuit of older people, driving a vast antiaging industry, advice books with titles that promise to turn back the clock, and Botox-esque businesses running into the billions?

To some extent the shift began with changes at the other end of the age spectrum. In the latter part of the nineteenth century and early decades of the twentieth, American society started recognizing childhood as a distinct life stage, a viewpoint reinforced by innovations like universal schooling and the creation of pediatrics as a specialty, along with the establishment of institutions like orphanages, high schools, even the Boy Scouts. Then came child labor laws and other legal strictures around the age one could enter the military, be employed, smoke cigarettes, and get married. Marketers entered the fray as well, ultimately creating categories like "toddlers" and later "teens"—and later yet, "tweens."

"Standardization spilled over into many different facets of life," according to Brown University historian Howard Chudacoff, author of the definitive book on the history of age awareness and segregation in America, *How Old Are You?* Chudacoff explains that an industrial mind-set—moving from standardizing the means of production to standardizing every other aspect of life—transformed education and other institutions into age-graded experiences. It was all done in the name of efficiency.

This approach continued apace in education, more and more finely separating young people to the point where older youth and younger ones rarely interacted during the school day. Meanwhile, this same radical reconceptualization and reorganization was happening at the other end of the age spectrum, with older people.

Later life went from being considered a natural part of the life cycle—indeed a divinely blessed one—to being deemed a medical condition, an incurable malady to be diagnosed, treated, and managed. In the process, older people themselves were transformed from admired icons to infirm and presumed incompetent individuals, unable to keep up with the quickening pace of assembly-line America. Institutions like nursing homes sprang up to warehouse these human artifacts on the periphery of society. Later they would be joined by other more affirmative but similarly age-segregating creations, such as senior centers and retirement communities.

Separated, older people were viewed increasingly as useless drains on the economy, on families, and on our collective resources.

The enactment of Social Security in the 1930s itself had an impact, hardening the definition of old age. The number sixty-five was established as the official eligibility age for benefits, in the process helping set the definition of being over the hill. Never mind that the number was picked virtually out of the air by a group of young New Dealers scrambling to get the legislation shaped and enacted under dire Depression circumstances.

Sixty-five was based on the eligibility age of the Prussian military pension, enacted in the 1870s by Otto von Bismarck, who was convinced the state would never need to pay a single pension. (He was in his late seventies at the time—something he must have forgotten.) Indeed, as Stanford economist John Shoven observes, we would never contemplate using 1935 dollars in twenty-first-century America without adjusting that number for inflation. Yet we treat the 1935 definition of old age as if it were an eternal verity.

The implications of expanded longevity were foreshadowed by Ida May Fuller, a retired legal secretary from Ludlow, Vermont, who, on January 31, 1940, become the first American to receive a Social Security check. She would go on to live past her one hundredth birthday, to witness the Beatles' invasion of America and the landing of a man on the moon. For her $24.75 in Social Security payments, she received a grand total of $22,888.92, enough of a discrepancy to put a deep chill in the hearts of fiscal hawks warning about the financial consequences of an older population.

Although Fuller was clearly on the outer edge of longevity in her time, by the postwar period the question of what to make of retirement and older people was becoming a far more unsettling and urgent one. In his address to the United Auto Workers 1949 conference in Milwaukee, for example, UAW president Walter Reuther captured the purpose gap that was beginning to emerge.

Reuther described the growing retiree population as "too old to work, too young to die," a group all too often consigned to an awkward yet extended land of limbo at the end of American life spans.

NOT SEGREGATION, INTEGRATION

By the mid-1950s the purpose gap captured by Reuther's characterization was, if anything, becoming even more deeply felt. In the words of eminent urbanist Lewis Mumford, "Probably at no period and in no culture have the old ever been so completely rejected as in our own country, during the last generation."

Writing in *Architectural Record* in 1956—as the first denizens of Youngtown were settling in—Mumford painted a woeful picture. "As their numbers have increased their position has worsened," he wrote. Mumford pointed to the dissolution of the three-generation family, arguing that "the aged find their lives progressively meaningless and empty, while their days ironically lengthen." The years that have been added to their life spans "have come, unfortunately, at the wrong end."

Mumford's piece was titled "For Older People: Not Segregation but Integration." It focused on how housing and community design together conspired to marginalize older people, shunting elders into age-segregated enclaves that cut them off from younger generations and from any sense of purpose. "To cause the aged to spend all their time glued to a television set is to damn them prematurely to a second childhood," he wrote. His main culprits were "specialization, mechanization, institutionalization, in a word, segregation," ideas that seemed efficient on the surface but that led, in his view, to the equivalent of "early euthanasia."

For all Mumford's warnings, the trend he decried was about to accelerate, indeed to define fully the latter phases of life. Already marketers from the financial services industry, eager to encourage Americans to think more positively about retirement, had started a massive advertising campaign portraying this period in life as a time of freedom and leisure.

But it was left for the real estate developers to marry age segregation and the ideal of a second youth, transforming retirement into a centerpiece of the American dream, one that would endure for more than half a century.

INVENTING THE GOLDEN YEARS
One of the four million viewers watching Dave Garroway's 1957 segment on Youngtown was Del Webb, the owner of the New York

Yankees and a developer of major projects throughout the emerging West. Webb was so intrigued by what was happening at Youngtown that he dispatched one of his associates, Tom Breen, to Clearwater, Florida—a naturally occurring retirement enclave—to talk with older people and find out what they thought of the idea.

Breen hitched a ride with a friend heading to Florida and proceeded to interview a string of seniors on park benches. What he heard left him convinced that the idea of an age-segregated, leisure-focused community for older adults might have considerable appeal, far beyond the 125 homes then dotting Youngtown.

Webb was captivated by Breen's account, and over the next three years, he would invest some $2 million (in 1950s dollars) into his own retirement community, Sun City. It was to be built on a dusty cotton field adjacent to Youngtown.

Webb—who became one of the preeminent shapers of American leisure in the postwar period—was the grandson of an English evangelist on one side and the man who spearheaded the creation of California's agricultural irrigation system on the other. And Webb himself proved both a gifted proselytizer and a master builder.

He is credited with inventing the motel. He turned Major League baseball into a business while owning the Yankees from 1946 to 1964, a period when they won ten world championships. He shaped Las Vegas. In the film *Bugsy*, it is Del Webb's Flamingo that Bugsy Siegel underwrites. (In real life, when Webb learned of Siegel's mob ties, the gangster succeeded in calming Webb by telling him, "Don't worry— we only kill each other.")

Moral judgments were, in any case, not something that concerned Webb much. During World War II, he built Japanese internment camps in California, and when challenged about those projects, he simply replied, "A job's a job."

For all his remaking of leisure in mid-twentieth-century America, Webb's influence is perhaps most profoundly seen in the realm of retirement. He coined the phrase "the golden years." And he, more than anyone else, established a whole new kind of social institution—the sunshine city for seniors, defined by leisure, recreation, and the notion of recapturing one's lost youth. It's true that Youngtown was first and that Big Ben Schleifer had the original idea, but Webb and Ross Cortese, who opened Leisure World in the early 1960s, were able to take the idea to a far greater scale and prominence, to imprint it on the American imagination.

Webb's unique genius was in managing to integrate two trends ascendant in the 1960s: the rejection of older people and the obsession with youth culture. Like Ben Schleifer, Webb set out to create not just a housing development but a separate world—overflowing with golf courses, shuffleboard courts, and swimming pools—where older people could be young again. A trip back to summer camp, a refuge, or as the Webb Company press releases put it, "a year-round vacation." (Think of it as a low-tech attempt at the fountain of youth, compared to Silicon Valley's high-tech version today.)

Still, there was trepidation in advance of Sun City's opening on January 1, 1960. The preceding evening, Webb's lieutenants gathered for dinner at Manuel's Place, a Mexican restaurant in Peoria, Arizona. There was much unease about the following morning's opening. The company had sunk a vast sum into the community of 1950s tract houses seemingly far from civilization. Even Phoenix felt far away. What if nobody showed up? Finally, Owen Childress, the manager in charge of sales voiced what was on all their minds: "How am I going to get a thirty-year mortgage on a guy who is sixty-five years old?"

By daybreak the next morning, long lines of cars were already forming into what would become the longest traffic jam in state history, ultimately stretching for two miles. That weekend one hundred thousand people in all showed up. Webb built it, and they came—and continued to come.

Today, the original Sun City has nearly forty thousand residents (and eight golf courses, not to mention a pair of bowling alleys). Sun Cities exist in eighteen states around the country. A senior housing industry still peddling the essential ingredients Schleifer pioneered and Webb mastered features annual revenues in the many billions. And the golden-years ideal that they embody has long stood as the default position for later life, the definition of success.

MAKING THE NATURAL UNNATURAL

Why did people flock to Sun City—and why do some keep flocking to age-segregated housing? I don't think skirting school taxes is the sole, or even most significant, factor. I don't even think the desire to live with same-age peers is ultimately about avoiding the noise, mess, and fuss of kids. I believe it has a lot more to do with finding community— and with the appeal of recapturing a sense of youthfulness in a society obsessed with youth.

Francis FitzGerald, in her Pulitzer Prize–winning book *Cities on a Hill,* observes that the whole illusion of a second childhood peddled by places like Sun City is predicated on the absence of children. *If everyone is old, then no one is old.* Actual children constitute the intrusion of reality and the upending of the eternal-youth fantasy.

For that reason, the definition of retirement as a life among same-age peers has always contained a disturbing underbelly—radical age segregation. Separation by age made a strange kind of sense in the context of 1950s America, which so thoroughly rejected older people, leaving them with nothing of importance to do. But the "solution" brought with it a new set of problems.

That underbelly was on excruciating display in 1997, when once again Youngtown found itself in the national spotlight. This time, the community wasn't the subject of a fawning Dave Garroway portrait of leisurely living in the desert. Forty years after opening its doors, Youngtown was generating headlines for its efforts to drive out an older couple accused of harboring their grandson.

Chaz Cope, the youth in question, needed asylum from an abusive stepfather and had no place else to turn. His Youngtown-resident grandparents paid $300 to apply for an exemption from the community's harsh age restrictions so Chaz could stay with them while completing high school. They were rejected. Indeed, for their high crime, Youngtown and its residents charged the couple $100 a day for violating its commitment to older-only life. A sign was planted on their lawn, in *Scarlet Letter*–like fashion, informing passersby of the offense.

Community leaders even circulated damning accounts (untrue ones, it would turn out) of the youth's transgressions. Rather than expressing remorse, Youngtown officials crowed to the *Arizona Republic* that they had expelled some three hundred young families during the first half of the decade. Indeed, the town's police officer was known to follow area school buses to ensure no children were being dropped off in Youngtown.

Describing these developments, the *New York Times* wrote: "Fresh-faced and direct, 16-year-old Chaz Cope would seem to be the ideal poster boy for this Phoenix suburb of sunshine and orange trees. Instead, this retirement community sees him as human contraband." No kids in Youngtown, the paper noted, but dogs were allowed.

After the Chaz Cope controversy, Arizona's state attorney general, Grant Woods, began looking into Youngtown's age restrictions, an investigation that led to overturning those rules.

Although federal housing laws ban a wide array of discrimination, they allow for age discrimination. Communities like Youngtown and Sun City, and hundreds more like them, are able to remain restricted senior-citizen colonies if 80 percent of the households have at least one resident over fifty-five and none of the permanent residents are under eighteen. Youngtown neglected to enshrine these rules officially into its charter and therefore was vulnerable to the attorney general's challenge.

The town was forced to open itself up to all ages.

Sun City—located just across 111th Avenue from the much smaller community—adhered to the letter of the law and wasn't required to become age integrated. Doubling down, Sun City even mounted an "age-police" force, described by the *New York Times* in an article entitled "In Haven for Over-55 Set, Age Police Hunt Violators Who Shriek or Toddle."

The article begins, "From behind the wheel of his minivan, Bill Szentmiklosi scours the streets of Sun City in search of zoning violations like unkempt yards and illegal storage sheds. Mostly, though, he is on the lookout for that most egregious of all infractions: children."

The price of segregation, it seems, is eternal vigilance.

Last summer when I visited Youngtown and its historical society, the town's librarian, Heidi Speed, took me afterward to the adjoining public library. The remodeled building is staffed by a pair of older white women, just what you might expect to see in the old Youngtown. But there's a difference today. When I arrived, a young Latino family was checking out books, interacting with the older residents. Just behind their desks, the library boasts young adult and children's sections. The town newspaper advertises youth sports leagues and family events. Police cars no longer trail school buses.

As I walked out into the blinding July light to await my ride to the airport, I felt as if I'd just witnessed something akin to grass popping up through cracks in a concrete sidewalk. The removal of age restrictions at this, the very first of all such communities, had brought with it new life.

I suspected that Big Ben Schleifer, the idealist from New York with images of a kibbutz in mind, might have approved—so long as home prices were affordable, of course.

SWIMMING UPSTREAM

The perils and prevalence of age segregation are by no means confined to the past, to Arizona and Florida, to Sun Cities and Leisure Worlds, to these monuments to age apartheid and the enduring allure of extended youth.

Demographer Richelle Winkler finds that age segregation in America today is often as deep-seated as racial segregation. Her research shows that in some parts of the country, old and young are roughly as segregated as Hispanics and whites. In another US study, about a third of people over fifty-five report that they reside in communities primarily made up of same-age peers.

"I think we're in the midst of a dangerous experiment," says Cornell University professor Karl Pillemer. "This is the most age-segregated society that's ever been. Vast numbers of younger people are likely to live into their 90s without contact with older people. As a result, young people's view of aging is highly unrealistic and absurd."

US senator Ben Sasse from Nebraska argues that separating the generations impoverishes the lives of old and young alike, bemoaning "age-segregated ghettos" and the negative consequences for community, maturity, faith, wisdom, and meaning. Most of all, he believes the absence of elders inhibits the character development of young people.

There are other negative effects of age segregation, as well. Without proximity, friendships don't easily form across the generations. Another study discovered that a mere 6 percent of people over sixty discussed "important matters" with nonfamily members younger than thirty-six.

Why does that matter? One of the chief reasons is that it contributes to loneliness, which has been described as the single most significant public health issue of our time by former surgeon general Vivek Murthy—equivalent in its adverse impact to smoking fifteen cigarettes a day. Older people and younger people, research shows, are the two groups most cut off from meaningful connection and most susceptible to the consequences of social isolation.

Over the past few years, I've come face to face with the widespread prevalence of this problem as my father—suffering from diabetes and dementia—bounced from one Philadelphia-area nursing home to another.

In the early months of 2017, I flew to Philadelphia with my wife and our three young boys to visit my father at one such place, a highly rated nursing home in the northeast section of the city. As we drove from the airport in our rental car, past the hospital where I was born, the religious congregation we attended, and the site where my dad and I once watched the Phillies play Sunday-afternoon doubleheaders, I tuned the radio to WXPN, the public radio station where I'd hosted a show in the 1980s.

The station that morning was playing blues, folk, and country music. As luck would have it, about ten minutes before we arrived to see my father, the DJ selected John Prine's song "Hello in There," about loneliness in later life. No matter how many times I've heard the song, Prine's lyrics still haunt.

> Ya' know that old trees just grow stronger
> And old rivers grow wilder ev'ry day
> Old people just grow lonesome
> Waiting for someone to say, "Hello in there, hello."

It was a fitting prelude to what awaited us. The facility was clean and safe, to be sure. After going through security at the entrance, we headed down a long corridor to the nursing unit, using hand sanitizer before crossing through another set of double doors, to find my father sitting at a table, slumped over, face-planted, with his glasses askew. Dozens of other men and women shared the room, but there was little social interaction.

Most striking: everyone was over seventy, except the staff.

As we filed in with our three boys, then ages seven, nine, and eleven, it was as if we'd arrived from some distant planet. The residents reached out to touch the children. The abject age segregation on display was all the more striking in the context of my father's own life. A former teacher and school administrator with a natural gift for connecting with children, he picked up his head and beamed when he saw his three young grandsons who had come from the other side of the country.

When my father took early retirement from the School District of Philadelphia—not because he was tired of working in education but because an incentive package to induce the exit of older and higher-paid employees made continuing to work financially disadvantageous—he became a substitute teacher, continuing to do that work into his eighties. He spent his "golden years" with young people in the classroom and outside it, also organizing track meets for elementary school students as a volunteer.

How could someone who thrived in the presence of the younger generation end up in an institution utterly bereft of children? And how could it be that there were so few available options for anything else?

In a single century we'd gone from one of the most age-integrated nations on earth to its mirror opposite. And in the process, we transformed the ideal for later life into an embrace of a second youth, at least for those who could hang on. In the end, culture and institutions lined up to radically reroute the river of life.

If biology flows downhill, we were left swimming upstream.

Chapter 4

AN ARMY FOR YOUTH

In the fall of 1997, I found myself driving my bright-blue Volkswagen Beetle between San Francisco and Palo Alto, on Highway 101 South, seated next to my hero, John W. Gardner. It was late at night, but John—eighty-five at the time—was nattily dressed in a *Mad Men*–era gray suit. A fedora sat neatly on his lap.

John and I were returning from a fateful meeting with top leaders of a billion-dollar foundation that would end up making a major investment in a new program called Experience Corps. I would be its cofounder, John would be the founding board member, and together we would work to create a domestic Peace Corps–like program, engaging older people to help the next generation thrive. It would be an attempt to create an army for youth. The foundation president agreed to provide the support on John's recommendation—describing him as the closest thing to infallibility in philanthropy.

John's idea for Experience Corps grew out of his time as secretary of health, education, and welfare (HEW), the lone Republican in Lyndon Johnson's administration. It was a sign of a different era that Johnson didn't even know Gardner's party affiliation when selecting him. As they walked out to announce the appointment, the president turned to Gardner and asked, "You are a Democrat, aren't you?" To which Gardner replied, "I'm a man who loves his country."

While at HEW, Gardner implemented Medicare, the Older Americans Act, and the Elementary and Secondary Education Act, all landmarks of public policy. Although only in his early fifties at the time, he'd already landed on the cover of *Time* magazine (five years after Del Webb graced the same cover, against a background of shuffleboard courts). Gardner had also been awarded the Presidential Medal of Freedom, the highest civilian honor an American can win, for his leadership of the Carnegie Corporation and his work helping to create PBS, the White House Fellows program, and many other significant innovations. His fellow winners of the 1964 Presidential Medal of Freedom: Walt Disney, Carl Sandburg, Aaron Copland, John Steinbeck, IBM founder Tom Watson, civil rights icon A. Philip Randolph, T. S. Eliot, Helen Keller, Willem de Kooning, and Lewis Mumford. Not bad company.

Yet John's most significant and enduring work lay ahead. In addition to being one of the architects of the Great Society, Gardner founded Common Cause to fight for campaign finance reform, with the slogan "Everyone is organized but the people." He had his hand in so many other groundbreaking efforts that the *New York Times* called him "the father of invention." There was a movement to draft him to run for president in 1968, but, as Gardner once told me, he lacked the ambition.

John came from modest means, growing up as the son of a single mother in Southern California but making it to Stanford, where he set Pacific-coast swimming records and met his wife, Aida, a visiting student from Guatemala.

The Experience Corps idea grew out of Gardner's travels during his HEW years, between 1965 and 1968, a time when many older people were being lifted out of deep poverty. Nearly 40 percent of the elderly had been living below the poverty line in the early 1960s, but the combination of expanding Social Security and enacting Medicare led to stunning improvements in their economic and health status.

Yet Gardner's visits around the country revealed deeper needs still unmet, most of all "the need to be needed." He recalled visiting a public housing project in Chicago, on one floor meeting a single mother with children in need of support and two floors above talking with an older woman in her apartment, socially isolated and crippled by loneliness. Why not bring need and resources together in a way that benefited both?

After leaving public service, John gathered his HEW speeches and writings into the 1968 book, *No Easy Victories.* Nestled among chapters on "A Just Society," "The Life and Death of Institutions," and "The Pursuit of Meaning" was one "On Aging," which suggested that later life might be the time when individuals made some of their most important contributions to society and to the development of future generations. (I once told John I had found a weather-beaten copy of the book at a library sale. He in turn told me he'd heard from Dwight Eisenhower's personal secretary that the book was on Eisenhower's night table when the former president died. Gardner beamed—until he read the liner notes Eisenhower had scrawled. One read, "This chapter is going nowhere!")

Gardner believed there was "a cruel and ironic contradiction" in the lives of older people. They could look forward to more and more years of life and health, yet "never before have they been so firmly shouldered out of every significant role in life—in the family, in the world of work and in the community."

Gardner saw "purpose in life" as the most important and neglected challenge facing these individuals, urging "more imaginative attempts" to supply work and volunteer opportunities for older people and highlighting efforts like Foster Grandparents and the Green Thumb program, the latter involving older people in environmental efforts. "We have barely begun to scratch the surface of such possibilities," he wrote, arguing that there was great promise in mobilizing a corps "patterned after the Peace Corps and VISTA that would serve the community and give older citizens something significant to do."

These efforts could be part-time or full-time, John noted; the structure wasn't critical. The most important thing was the fit, the pieces of a jigsaw puzzle that were designed to come together. "The possibilities are limitless because of the serious shortages in every one of the so-called helping professions," he presciently wrote. "If you set yourself the task of identifying these fields of human activity that cannot be automated—the areas in which humans cannot be replaced by machines—you will find that many involve the helping fields. You can automate some of the activities a nurse performs, but the human element is of the essence. The usefulness of a companion to an elderly person is not just in the tasks performed but in the human interaction."

Why not bring together people who need help and people who want to be helpful in ways that rely upon and build essential human connection?

I met Gardner twenty-five years after he'd written this essay, at a Carnegie-sponsored conference on the after-school hours. He was the keynote speaker on the subject of building community, and he gave an unsentimental account. It was true, he declared, that both family and community had changed in significant ways: "To be blunt about it, neither will ever be wholly reinstated in its old form." But it was time to face up to change, he said, dispense with yearning for a mythic past, and move forward in new ways. Besides, Gardner added wryly, it was generally unwise to be nostalgic about anything unless you were absolutely certain it wouldn't be coming back.

As I first recounted in the book *Prime Time*, an hour after the speech on community, I found myself heading straight toward Gardner in a crowded corridor. He was alone, and I mustered the courage to introduce myself. Talking fast, I also managed to interject that I had written a background paper for Carnegie on the role older Americans might play in assisting the younger generation. He listened patiently and nodded occasionally, while mostly looking down at the ground. Because of his silence, I was beginning to regret having imposed myself, as a steady stream of conference-goers brushed past us in both directions.

Just as I was convinced that Gardner was simply being polite, he reached into a brown leather briefcase, rummaged about, and fished out a typewritten three-page paper from 1988 labeled "The Experience Corps." (This scene would repeat itself again and again over the coming years, as we began working closely together. I would raise an issue, convinced that I had happened on some formidable insight, and John would produce, as if by magic and with no fanfare whatsoever, a beautifully crafted treatise fully explicating the subject.)

John believed Experience Corps could unleash the time, talent, and know-how of older Americans to revitalize civil society. "We believe, without being immodest," he wrote in the paper, "that the large numbers of us over age 65 constitute a rich reservoir of talent, experience and commitment potentially available to the society. . . . We know the conventional view is that society owes its older citizens something, and we would be foolish to quarrel with that. But we owe something, too, and this is in one sense our 'operation give-back.'" Giving back hardly precluded getting back, and Gardner envisioned Experience Corps as an opportunity for continued learning and growth in later life, "a great adventure."

To establish Experience Corps, John and I worked over the coming years with a visionary geriatrician from Johns Hopkins, Dr. Linda Fried, now dean of the Mailman School of Public Health at Columbia, and Tom Endres, then head of Senior Corps and formerly the director of the senior service programs in Maine, where he, too, came to know and love Aggie and Louise. Over those years, John went from a hero to a mentor to a close friend.

Most of our conversations in the late 1990s were about the practicalities of creating Experience Corps or forming a new organization to house it. So I was determined to make the most of my late-night ride with Gardner in 1997 as I drove him back to his home near the Stanford campus, where he'd moved to teach leadership at the university's Graduate School of Business.

Ultimately, I posed the question I most wanted to know: What did John feel was his proudest achievement? I wasn't sure that I would get an answer. Although he was always patient with me and willing to answer questions about the past, I learned that Gardner was much more interested in talking about the future—the future he would never see. But this time he answered quickly: his book *Self-Renewal*, which was published in 1963 and would go on to become a best seller and a classic of American positive thinking.

I became so absorbed in the conversation with Gardner that I neglected to realize, speeding along on the nighttime freeway, that the traffic ahead of us had come to a sudden halt. A mass of flashing taillights was rapidly accumulating, and I belatedly slammed on my brakes. The Volkswagen swerved sharply to the left, then to the right, before coming to rest inches from the vehicle in front of us. The entire time Gardner—hands firmly planted on the dashboard—was repeating a single phrase: "Oh my God."

The phrase repeating in my head? "You're killing a national treasure!"

In the years ahead, John always found polite excuses to avoid getting in a car with me, but our friendship blossomed nonetheless.

EXPERIENCE CORPS

Experience Corps drew heavily on the broad strokes Gardner had outlined in his paper. To build our army for youth, we married his ideas and the name he coined with what I'd learned from years of talking to innovative Foster Grandparents directors. "If you could redesign the program in ways that would be most effective without concern for existing rules and regulations," I asked them repeatedly, "what would you do?"

Linda Fried, an expert on well-being in later life, contributed insights from the fields of medicine and public health. She also brought a desire to encourage, even prescribe, social engagement and purpose to her older patients, who all too often were missing both. From his government perch, Tom Endres added deep knowledge about service programs for older people and $1 million in federal funding for innovation. A national competition among Foster Grandparents and

RSVP (a federal senior volunteer network) programs was held to pick five locations to pilot the new model.

Our primary goal was simple: to mobilize older people to help low-income children thrive. Experience Corps focused on elementary schools and, ultimately, on helping students read by the third grade. If it succeeded, we felt that the program could be reproduced widely in grade schools everywhere. Teams of ten to fifteen Experience Corps members were deployed in mostly inner-city schools to create a critical mass of older adults at each location, both to influence the climate of the school and to provide a "family" of Experience Corps members, replacing collegial bonds from the workplace and offering the presence of mutual support.

We hoped that by demonstrating the effectiveness of the new model, we could help reform and modernize Foster Grandparents. To that end, we lifted the restriction on Experience Corps members' income so the program was open to anyone committed to serving, regardless of financial status. And we asked each recruit to pledge to a minimum of fifteen hours a week. We hoped to engage older people who wanted to make Experience Corps a centerpiece of their life and who were determined to have a significant impact on the education of young people.

We also hoped to age-integrate national service. A few years earlier, Bill Clinton had created AmeriCorps with the idea of engaging young people in their communities. We envisioned younger *and* older people being the twin bulwarks of the national service movement. A Ford Foundation report on the subject—written by Richard Danzig, who would go on to become secretary of the navy, and Peter Szanton, a professor at Harvard's Kennedy School of Government—bolstered our view. Danzig and Szanton found that for all the value of service by young people, it was older folks who had "more to give and more to get from national service than any other group."

We hoped Experience Corps would be the beginning of something vast, not only revitalizing Foster Grandparents but expanding it so

that it became a defining American institution. We winnowed down
the applications and picked five sites: Philadelphia; New York; Minne-
apolis; Portland, Oregon; and Port Arthur, Texas (a small Gulf Coast
city that's also the birthplace both of the singer Janis Joplin and former Dallas Cowboys' coach Jimmy Johnson).

Gardner wrote the first-ever outside editorial in AARP's magazine,
calling its members to join Experience Corps and listing my personal
mailbox as the place they could send letters of inquiry. It was soon
overflowing. And AARP chapters in the five pilot cities sent mailings
to their local members, putting their trusted imprimatur on the enterprise. The organization's support was invaluable in providing legiti-
macy and in getting our new venture off the ground.

Soon we had five pilots under way across the country—and a set of
big questions loomed: Would anybody show up? Would schools be willing to make use of these individuals? Would the promised outcomes
actually be realized?

Things started slowly. Most school principals we approached were
skittish, but in every city a small group raised their hands, eager to
host such a corps. By the end of the first year, momentum was building, and it kept building. Two years in, there was a sense that something magical, and important, was under way.

But as the program established itself and expanded, funders and
potential funders wanted evidence of its effectiveness. Eventually, a
group of private foundations, and later government sources, invested
millions in a major research effort to try to understand the benefits to
all those involved. Linda Fried's team at Johns Hopkins was joined by
a parallel effort led by Professor Nancy Morrow-Howell at Washington University in St. Louis.

Like the Big Brothers Big Sisters study, the Experience Corps
research showed the program was having a significant and meaningful impact. The Washington University team, working with analysts
from Mathematica Policy Research, tested results for more than eight
hundred students in the first, second, and third grades in twenty-three

schools in three cities. They discovered in a random-assignment, controlled study that the students who worked with Experience Corps members scored *60 percent* better than peers on a pair of essential literacy skills: reading comprehension and the sounding out of new words.

What does that mean exactly, beyond honing better reading skills? As the Washington University researchers explained, having support from Experience Corps members was equivalent to being in a classroom with 40 percent fewer students, at a fraction of the cost of reducing class size. Linda Fried and a team of Johns Hopkins researchers produced significant and complementary findings, employing an exceptionally rigorous approach to studying outcomes for 1,194 K–3 students in a half-dozen urban elementary schools in low-income Baltimore neighborhoods.

In the Johns Hopkins research, third-grade students performed better on the Maryland School Performance Assessment Program than peers in control schools without Experience Corps. And these academic results were matched by important behavioral benefits. Referrals to the principal's office for behavioral problems went down dramatically, between 30 and 50 percent, in the Baltimore schools with Experience Corps members. Other research showed that both teachers and principals gave Experience Corps exceptionally high marks—93 percent of teachers surveyed said their students' reading and writing skills improved as a result of the Experience Corps members' support.

As with Foster Grandparents, the money spent benefited both the students and the older adults. The Johns Hopkins researchers, along with colleagues at Columbia and UCLA, uncovered important gains in physical and mental well-being compared to a similar group of older people not involved in Experience Corps. Those with arthritis had less pain; others with diabetes required fewer medications to keep their blood sugar under control.

There was even evidence from Michelle Carlson at Johns Hopkins School of Public Health suggesting that involvement in Experience

Corps had a positive impact on cognitive functioning. Linda Fried wrote in the *Atlantic* in 2014 that most volunteers who spent six months in the program dramatically improved their ability to solve complex problems. What's more, these Experience Corps members "showed new activation in areas of the brain involved with complex problem-solving, compared with a control group with a similar level of education who did not participate."

Experience Corps members, she reported, felt the program dusted off the cobwebs in their brains.

BEYOND THE NUMBERS

We devoted a great deal of time, money, and careful analysis to research on Experience Corps. In the end, this examination revealed significant, quantifiable gains for students, older adults, and school climate. Still, when I think about the importance of the program, a single photograph comes to mind. Taken by Alex Harris, the founder of Duke University's Center for Documentary Studies, it's a picture from the playground of a Philadelphia elementary school in the Powelton Village neighborhood, then a down-on-its-heels West Philadelphia area in the shadows of the University of Pennsylvania and Drexel University.

It's a spring day. An Experience Corps member, a tall African American woman in a print dress, with reading glasses clutched in her left hand, is swinging a jump rope held at the other end by a student in cornrows. Floating above the rope at the height of her leap, dressed entirely in white (sandals, pants, shirt), is a little girl, her head turned to the side, eyes partly closed, in a state that can only be described as bliss. The three of them are suspended in the moment, as another student looks on and rows of public housing stretch out in the background. Beneath them their shadows are outlined on the cracked pavement.

The engagement so evident in the scene helps explain findings like the physical and mental health benefits to the older members. But there is much more on display. The essence of Experience Corps from the beginning could be found in a generation of African Americans, particularly African American women, who were largely from the same neighborhoods as the students, places like Powelton Village. Many had gone as youngsters to the schools where they now served. They were, essentially, bastions of social capital.

To appreciate the significance of these individuals and the role they played, it's useful to see them in the context of evolving African American neighborhoods in post–World War II America. Harvard sociologist William Julius Wilson argues that these role models were instrumental in upholding the importance of education, family, and community solidarity. They're gone now, Wilson contends, having departed for the suburbs as racism in housing restrictions began to loosen. Young people growing up in these neighborhoods today, he says, no longer have access to the stability and oversight they provided.

Without necessarily contesting Wilson's argument that there's a downside to out-migration of better educated individuals from urban neighborhoods, a number of leading ethnographers studying these neighborhoods present a more nuanced picture. They find that many of the pillars Wilson extols still remain in communities but no longer play the role they did with previous generations.

Anthropologist Elijah Anderson of Yale University labels these figures "old heads," and in *Streetwise*, his landmark study of inner-city Philadelphia neighborhoods, he characterizes the old head/youth relationship as "essentially one of mentor and protégé." According to Anderson, for generations, the male old head was an essential asset of African American neighborhoods, critical to the stability of these communities and a bridge to jobs in the blue-collar economy.

Female old heads, he observes, played "an important fictive kinship role of extra parent or surrogate mother." In the words of one woman, quoted by Anderson, "The way I feel about it . . . 'I love all children'; if you don't love somebody else['s] children, you don't love [your] own."

General Colin Powell, the former secretary of state and founding chair of America's Promise Alliance, describes this web of support in similar terms, asking, "How do children gain expectations to put in their hearts and souls? They get it from the adults in their lives." He says he got it as a child growing up in the Bronx, not from one person but from a combination of parents, aunts, uncles, ministers, and teachers. He argues that what mentors do for children "is to pass on a hundred previous generations of experience."

Powell passed a procession of caring adults on the way home from school each day. These older women and men offered support but also were quick to report unruly behavior to parents. "Everybody talks about the speed of the Internet," Powell says. "Well, nothing can compare to the speed of the Aunt-net in the South Bronx."

From his research, Anderson concludes that a combination of factors has contributed to the decline in the ability of old heads to play their traditional roles. It often became too dangerous to do so from the porches of changed neighborhoods, and the decline in public trust created additional wariness about intervening in the lives of other people's children on the streets.

Spending time with Experience Corps members in Powelton Village and other largely African American neighborhoods in Philadelphia, and the many other cities where Experience Corps grew, I felt like I was watching the second coming of the old heads (or the Aunt-net). *They'd moved from the porch to the school.* In a sign of cultural and community resilience, these individuals had discovered a new platform to play traditional roles, a new way to do old things.

In many cities, some 85 percent of Experience Corps members were African American and Latino, and the African American members in particular were a bridge not only to past community roles but to the civil rights generation. Getting to know the Experience Corps members in Philadelphia—where I'd attended public schools—was a chance to understand aspects of my racially segregated hometown that weren't visible to me while I was growing up.

For all these divides, I found the Experience Corps members in Philadelphia, and really everywhere, to be enormously warm and open. One of my favorites was Harold Allen, a man who grew up as one of the few African Americans in an Italian neighborhood in South Philadelphia. He spent the first part of his life as an active civil rights campaigner before settling into a job with the city's water department. After retiring with a good pension, Allen took on a second career counseling the incarcerated. Motivated by the desire to influence young people before they ended up in prison, he spent his next phase of "retirement" with Experience Corps.

I remember Harold telling me, "Patience does come with age. . . . Now, you're less self-involved. You're able to look back in retrospect and understand better what happened. And death is something that you come to realize is part of life. It is not something you dread. . . . But you want to leave good memories of yourself, and you hope to leave something behind that's worthwhile."

Harold's work at Taylor Elementary School in North Philadelphia was not a tough sell. "The children are so starved for attention that they just latch on," he said. "When you arrive, they run to you, and when you miss a day, right away, it's 'Why weren't you here?'"

Allen's description reminds me of a story I heard from another Experience Corps member at Taylor School, a story that captures the mutuality of these bonds. Martha Jones woke up one gray, winter Philadelphia day feeling poorly. She turned off the alarm and contemplated remaining in bed. She pulled the covers over herself. But as Jones thought further, she kept returning to how much the children were counting on her presence. She went back and forth before ultimately deciding to get dressed, go downstairs, head out into the cold, and drive to the school.

Jones walked up the stairs to the classroom in the 1920s-era school building. As she was hanging up her coat, still not convinced she'd made the right decision, she could feel "these two little arms" reaching from behind to hug her, the arms of one of the little girls she'd been working with. I remember Jones telling me, "I'm short and they can reach me—and I was surprised." She laughed. "I got these two little arms around me. It just caught me off guard, but I was really moved by that. I said, 'Hey, somebody likes me!'"

We hear a lot today about the need to be needed, and the benefits of social connection to health and well-being in later life. I always think about that conversation with Martha Jones.

When I was interviewing Experience Corps members, it was clear to me that there was an ongoing debate among them about the program's goal. Was it a corps designed to bring the *experience* of older people—that experience of a hundred generations Colin Powell describes—to benefit young people, or was it a corps designed to provide older people meaningful and purposeful *experiences*? To which I'd say yes and yes.

And why, people often wondered, did younger and older get along so well?

That's a more complicated question. Writing an early essay about Experience Corps in Philadelphia, journalist Rob Gurwitt visited Rev. Cookie Bracey, pastor of the largely African American Mount Carmel United Methodist Church and an Experience Corps member at the school just down the street from her congregation. Bracey said she often wondered why "even unrelated children and old people seem to take to each other." Gurwitt answered with the comedian Sam Levenson's line: "The reason grandparents and grandchildren get along so well is that they have a common enemy"—parents. Bracey begged to differ, saying, "I think it's a God-given gift. . . . It's a mystery."

That mysterious love between generations had profoundly practical effects when it came to changing the culture of schools and neighborhoods. On my first visit to the Experience Corps team at Taylor, I recall the principal showing me that the school mailboxes were alphabetically organized, interspersing the Experience Corps members' boxes along with those of the teachers, administrators, counselors, and other employees. The members had become a fundamental part of the institution's fabric, not seen as occasional volunteers who showed up from time to time.

The same familiarity started appearing outside the school. Parents and children would be in the local Acme supermarket when the kids would encounter an Experience Corps member, run up, and hug them, yelling out, "Grandma!" At several Philadelphia schools, members came up with the idea of hosting parent breakfasts to draw those adults into the school when they came to drop off their children. In these instances, Corps members, not authority figures like the teachers or principals, served as bridges between the neighborhood and the school.

In Philadelphia and every other Experience Corps city I visited, corps members formed close bonds with the teacher whose classroom they worked in. Although it was never part of the formal design, Experience Corps members came to mentor teachers as much as students. They were often the only other adult in the classroom, sometimes establishing order when new teachers didn't yet know how but mostly providing emotional support and perspective.

And the bonds radiated laterally as well. Experience Corps members often became like family to one another, substituting for the work peers they no longer had, discussing the challenges of the job, and supporting each other in school and out, through illnesses and family crises and loss.

Decades later, I come away convinced that although Experience Corps was frequently characterized as a tutoring program aimed at helping kids read by grade three, really it was a relationship program, and not just for the kids—but for all those it touched.

The conventional wisdom is that the relationships provided a foundation for the tutoring help. Today I think that formulation has it backward. The reading lessons became the scaffolding around which a rich array of bonds could take hold. And these bonds weren't just a means to an end; they became an important end in and of themselves.

BREATHTAKING OPPORTUNITIES

Experience Corps today engages about twenty-three hundred older adults to help thirty-one thousand low-income children in more than twenty cities get on a path to success. Its scale hasn't yet reached the national service corps that John Gardner, Linda Fried, Tom Endres, and I dreamed of, but it is doing a great deal of good for children, older adults, schools, parents, teachers, and communities. In 2011, AARP, which had done so much to help Experience Corps get off the ground, adopted it, invested in it, and put it in a much stronger position to grow—which it continues to do today.

We set out to create an army for youth. We succeeded in creating something closer to a battalion, not the vast new institution to transform the role of older people in the lives of children, but a battalion nonetheless. Still, the forces that work against bringing innovation to scale, even successful innovation, are strong. Dollars for schools are scarce, and resources to recruit, train, and deploy service corps members and volunteers scarcer. Local and federal bureaucracies, inertia, the persistent undervaluing of contributions by older people—they all get in the way. Still, I hold tight to dreams of that cavalry coming over the hill.

We set out to demonstrate that older adults could improve students' reading skills and their own lives in the process. We succeeded, learning a great deal about the power of all the relationships created to change lives and to change the culture of an institution called school.

We set out to find new ways to do old things—new ways to connect the generations and to revive the village that raises children by engaging all the caring adults on the block. And we did so not to satisfy a nostalgic yearning for days gone by but because the world had changed. If we wanted the connections between generations to live on, we had to change, too.

I learned all those things and more from Experience Corps and from John Gardner. John's idea for Experience Corps was forged in the 1960s, when he first called for a domestic Peace Corps–like effort to mobilize older people. He would live another six years after Experience Corps was launched in the mid-1990s, until prostate cancer spread throughout his body, and he passed away just shy of his ninetieth birthday.

In those final half-dozen years, we launched Encore.org, the organization I still lead twenty years later, and we spent a lot of time together. Although he taught a popular course on leadership at Stanford's Graduate School of Business during that final phase of his life, John was in much less demand nationally, and it became easier to spend unhurried time with him. He would never admit it and was utterly allergic to feeling sorry for himself, but I think he felt a little forgotten during that period.

I remember the lift John got when he was invited to give the keynote at the thirty-fifth anniversary of the White House Fellows program, which he attended despite doctors' orders to the contrary. The program was one of his proudest achievements, and he returned—having spent time with Colin Powell and other fellows—with an extra bounce in his step. At the twentieth anniversary of another of his masterworks, Common Cause, Gardner joked about his speaking being an exercise in "ancestral deference," then went on to admit that he was "more conscious than ever of the passage of time."

He then told a story, funny but also revealing, about getting a call from his centenarian mother when he was close to eighty. His mother started out by saying, "Johnny, this whole aging thing has got me down." To which he responded, "But, Mom, you're doing great for your age. You've got all your faculties." She cut him off. "It's not me I'm talking about—it's you and your brother!"

As age and illness began to weigh heavily on him, John—always resilient—took a piece of construction paper, neatly folded it into a square, then inscribed on it a single word, "purpose," before taping the paper to the wall above his desk. The touchstone helped him get through his last year of life, his grandson told me. It helped him stay focused on what mattered most.

The final time I heard John speak publicly, shortly before his passing, he talked in very personal terms about roadblocks to renewal in the second half of life. "All my feelings about the release of human possibilities, all of my convictions about renewal," he said, "are offended by the widely shared cultural assumption that life levels off in one's forties and fifties and heads downhill, so that by sixty-five you are scrap-heap material."

Then he offered a closing plea, turning to look at all of us middle-agers listening raptly in the audience. "What I want for those youngsters in their forties and fifties is several more decades of vital learning and growth. And I want something even broader and deeper. I don't know whether I can even put it into words. What I want . . . is a long youthfulness of spirit. It doesn't seem much to ask—but it is everything."

The friendship with John was everything to me. To be honest, I never felt worthy of all the time he devoted to our work together and to our relationship. But I still think about him often, as I, too, am more conscious than ever of the passage of time.

In the end, when John finally passed away, I attended the memorial service for him at the Stanford Chapel. It was a vast crowd, filled with notables. As I entered, programs were being handed out by former senators Tim Wirth and Bill Bradley. On the back was a single quote from Gardner, taken from a speech he gave during the battles over Medicare in 1965: "America today faces breathtaking opportunities disguised as insoluble problems." There could be no better benediction for the multigenerational society, its soaring possibilities, and what that shift might mean for all ages.

But how to break through, to seize those opportunities? Experience Corps was, and is, an important step and a proof of concept. But how can we go beyond the contours of a program to reach into the lives of millions of people, not tens of thousands? How can we change the culture and the institutions—the places we live, learn, and work—that define our daily lives? How can we find that path to individual and social renewal so central to John Gardner's vision of Experience Corps—and of life?

Chapter 5

DREAMING AND SCHEMING

I grew up in a quadrant of Philadelphia that was, in the 1950s and 1960s, the chief destination for white people fleeing integration within the city's borders. More than half a million people lived there, mostly in modest neighborhoods of new tract housing. As a result, my high school had six thousand students in a building meant to accommodate half that number. A single student was African American; all the rest were white.

When I moved back to Philadelphia as an adult, I landed a half-dozen miles from my parents' home, in the Mt. Airy/Germantown neighborhood, the one part of the city that (mostly) welcomed integration. The area was one of the city's most beautiful neighborhoods as well. Instead of the cookie-cutter homes that marked my childhood, Mt. Airy was full of stone houses and older buildings dating back centuries, all adjoining the Wissahickon Creek, wooded parklands, and trails. Everyone knew the Weavers Way Food Co-Op, a cramped row house several blocks from my apartment where you could buy vegetables, cheese, and bulk goods.

I lived in an apartment building that was roughly half African American and half white. The African Americans were mostly middle aged or older, post office and government employees and hairdressers who'd lived in Mt. Airy for decades. The whites were primarily younger people, students and college-educated women and men starting out in their careers. There was a pervasive sense of community, despite outward differences. I don't know if I've ever felt more at home.

A mile away, an older woman was resisting a different kind of segregation. I never met her, but Maggie Kuhn, then in her late seventies, lived six blocks from my apartment. Forced by her employer, the Presbyterian Church, to retire at sixty-five, Kuhn founded the Gray Panthers in 1970 to fight ageism and age segregation. "When we are kept apart from those who will live on after us," Kuhn said, "we deprive ourselves and we also deprive the young." The group's motto: "Age and Youth in Action!"

Kuhn owned two homes in Germantown. She lived in one with her "family of choice," which included one married couple, a trio of single men, and a pair of single women, according to an early 1980s profile in the *New York Times*. Jews, Catholics, and Protestants—including a seminarian—were included in the household mix. Several were graduate students at the time.

A slender woman with white hair swept up in a bun and granny glasses, Kuhn got the idea for her multigenerational enclave in the early 1960s when her ailing mother took in a pair of University of Pennsylvania students to live with and care for her. By the time the Germantown enclave was up and running, Kuhn had become a leading voice on intergenerational housing, opening a nonprofit, the National Shared Housing Resource Center, on the main floor of one of her homes.

Kuhn minced no words in describing age-segregated retirement communities and senior facilities. "I think they're glorified playpens," she remarked in 1978. "While I admit that they help to keep elders safe, I don't like how they segregate older men and women from mainstream society." She continued, "In our modern society, there's too much emphasis placed on independence. As we live longer lives, I strongly believe we'd all be better off if we were more interdependent."

Kuhn was eager to match older people like herself, house rich but income poor (she had spent her entire life working for the YWCA and the Presbyterian Church), with younger people who couldn't afford to buy a home or pay high rents. A commonsense idea, it worked in Philadelphia in the 1970s and 1980s—and not just because of the economics. Kuhn told a reporter that the shared housing experiment exceeded her expectations. "We've grown to have very close and loving friendships that endure," she said. "We depend on each other, without being sentimental about it."

One of Kuhn's protégés at the time was Nancy Henkin, who later became the founder of the Intergenerational Center at Temple University and one of the great pioneers and innovators in this arena for decades. I recently asked Henkin about her relationship with Kuhn. They met when Nancy was starting a new job at Temple University's Institute on Aging and Kuhn was in the early stages of setting up her Germantown multigenerational living experiment. The two women, more than forty years apart in age, formed an indelible bond.

"It was 1979," Nancy told me. "I wanted to find ways to involve older people in the university, and I thought about starting an Elder-hostel program. And someone said, 'You should talk to Maggie Kuhn.' She was in Philadelphia, so I called her up, and I went to talk to her."

"Elderhostels are great," Kuhn told her, but too often the older people who attend classes on college campuses don't really interact with the younger ones. "There's a space there."

So Henkin developed an intergenerational learning retreat instead, bringing people from the age of thirteen to almost one hundred together to live in the dorms for five days each summer. "It was mixed racially, socioeconomically, educationally, and Maggie was our keynote speaker a few years in a row," Henkin said. "The retreat made me realize that people are really yearning for community and a way to connect with others. I began to think about what else we could do to start bringing generations together."

Over time, Henkin said Kuhn became "smaller and smaller in size, but not in fortitude and presence and personality, and she'd say—I'll never forget what she'd say—'Sit down here. Let's dream and scheme.'"

Although Kuhn had indomitable determination—she was described by the *New York Times* as a "diminutive militant"—Henkin remembers how slight she became in later life. Once, after attending a conference in New York City, Henkin hailed a cab with Kuhn in stormy weather. The winds were whipping about them, and Kuhn had to hang on to a lamppost to keep from being swept away. "Near the end," Henkin told me, "when I was going to see her, she was very frail. She was bent over. Her hands were gnarled. But she had a sparkle in her eyes, and she would still say, 'Let's dream and scheme.'"

Kuhn died in 1995 at the age of eighty-nine. As she requested, her epitaph states, "Here lies Maggie Kuhn under the only stone she left unturned."

THE INNOVATION IMPERATIVE

Over the past century, creative ideas have shaped aging, retirement, and longer lives in the United States. Presidents and policy wonks, with support from the people, created Social Security, Medicare, and the Older Americans Act. A retired high school principal named Ethel Percy Andrus founded AARP in 1958. And tens of thousands contributed to medical advances and new attitudes about fitness and healthy living.

There have been stunning benefits from all this invention. Older people went from the poorest age group of the population to the least poor. Lives lengthened dramatically. But many of the inventions over the past century—including retirement communities, senior centers, nursing homes, and assisted-living facilities—have likewise left us with a legacy of separation and segregation. Many of these ideas have been well intentioned and valuable in important ways, while at the same time rife with unfortunate and unintended consequences.

Where is the dreaming and scheming we need now? The innovation that will build on the genuine progress in extended life spans and economic security in ways that connect people across generations instead of separating them? That's what Maggie Kuhn and Nancy

Henkin were plotting and planning as they sat together in Kuhn's multigenerational house in Germantown.

And that's the question I was left thinking about in the aftermath of Experience Corps' initial phase, with all its progress and achievements and suggestions of promising ways forward. I still find myself haunted by a favorite quote from Thomas Mann: "There is at bottom only one problem in the world and this is its name. How does one break through? How does one get into the open? How does one burst the cocoon and become a butterfly?"

What will it take to burst the cocoon? Where are the new approaches capable of turning around all the separation and segregation that's been sown? Who is mustering the imagination needed to bring us together, at a level of creativity that rivals the imagination used over the past decades to split us apart? I wonder and worry about whether we will rise to this challenge.

There are, I'm pleased to report, some promising indications that we will. As I've traveled the country and the globe searching for seeds of change, I've noticed a quiet but steady growth in just the kind of innovation that's needed, even if it's often hidden in plain sight. I've been simultaneously struck by how many of these creative ideas are taking root in the central settings where we spend our lives—in housing, communities, educational institutions, and the workplace.

I believe these innovations offer a glimpse of how we can do better, often starting with a commonsense idea for solving a specific problem, then unfolding into something much richer.

Innovation often defies categorization, but I see three basic types of dreamers and schemers working to bring the generations together for mutual benefit: **inventors** who are dreaming up radical new ideas; **integrators** who are bringing existing institutions, like senior centers and preschools, together; and **infiltrators** who are typically injecting older or younger people into settings where you might not have found them previously.

The edges blur. But the fundamental feature is the same: the idea that we're better together.

THE INVENTORS

Inventors, to my mind, are creating something novel, even utopian. Their ideas may not be easily replicable, but they are groundbreaking, influential, even breathtaking.

The Treehouse Foundation in Easthampton, Massachusetts, fits squarely in the American tradition of utopian problem solving. It is practical idealism in the spirit of Maggie Kuhn's Germantown experiment in multigenerational living. Treehouse founder Judy Cockerton—a parent, foster parent, former teacher, and toy store owner—knew from her own experience that it wasn't possible for isolated foster families to give vulnerable kids all the support they needed. Drawing entirely on a single family's resources just wasn't sufficient.

Cockerton likewise believed that many people wanted to help foster kids thrive but weren't prepared to become foster parents themselves. So she set about developing a village where foster and adoptive families would get the supportive community they need and where older people could live among them, realize the chance to become surrogate grandparents, and find a rich network of peers along the way. Treehouse is—as Father Gregory Boyle, founder of Homeboy Industries in Los Angeles, describes his own work—in the "radical kinship" business, building a rich tapestry of ties between people who need each other but who might otherwise never find one another.

Cockerton took her inspiration from University of Illinois social work professor Brenda Eheart, who created Hope Meadows in 1994 on the grounds of a former air force base in Illinois. Eheart raised funds to buy a block of houses on the base and transform the dozens of units into homes for families raising foster kids and for elders happy to be part of their lives.

Eheart's brilliance is a variation on the architectural concept of *adaptive reuse,* a term for bringing old buildings back to life to serve new functions—think the former warehouse turned artist's loft. Eheart transformed a base aimed at training soldiers for war into an oasis designed to create bonds of love. And, in the process, you could say that she facilitated another form of adaptive reuse. Older people who were all too often regarded as obsolete became invaluable linchpins of community.

When conceiving of Hope Meadows, Brenda Eheart drew on her own experience growing up in a small town in upstate New York where older and younger people were deeply enmeshed in each other's lives. Indeed, Ted Koppel, then of ABC News, said Hope Meadows was "a town so old-fashioned it's new."

Against the backdrop of Mt. Tom in central Massachusetts, Treehouse has about one hundred residents—families in the process of adopting children from the public foster care system and a group of older (mostly) women and men. The families live in a dozen rental town houses. The older people (singles and some couples) occupy forty-eight senior cottages, interspersed among the other dwellings and designated as affordable housing for people over fifty-five.

The physical design of Treehouse is crafted to promote intergenerational connections and a small-town feel, with pathways and common areas facilitating day-to-day contact among residents. The senior bungalows have porches to encourage sociability. There's a library and a kitchen for communal cooking. The community center includes a heavily used dining hall for regular potlucks, movie nights, and community activities, including the TreeCat Cafe, which hosts musical performances and gives young people the chance to learn how to run a business.

One of the surprising benefits at Treehouse is the development of bonds that are both vertical, between generations, and horizontal, among the elders, who support each other in much the way that Experience Corps members do. Another feature of life at Treehouse, perhaps not fully grasped at its launch, is the presence of frailty and mortality. Cockerton explained to me that they'd lost almost a dozen elders since Treehouse started—a valuable and visible reminder of the cycle of life for young people.

While visiting Treehouse, I met Maureen Sinquez, who had previously lived with her husband in a retirement community in Florida. A nurse in her professional life, she had spent the last years in Florida caregiving as her husband succumbed to Alzheimer's. When he passed away, she decided to fill the void by coming to Treehouse.

Treehouse, Sinquez told me, offered an answer to what she had been missing in Florida. "I lived in a gated community . . . and the only laughter in that community was just a couple of times a month when the grandkids came, and I think they could only stay three or four days." The most prevalent sound was the low whir of golf carts. There was a prohibition on planting gardens. Most strikingly absent was the sound of children. At Treehouse, she said, "There's grass, there's laughter . . . it fills you up."

Listening to Sinquez and visiting Treehouse, I couldn't help but think of Youngtown and of Big Ben Schleifer. Both Judy Cockerton and Big Ben set out to create shining cities on the hill (or in the desert, as the case may be), albeit ones with very different goals. Del Webb took Big Ben's idea and made it widespread and mainstream. Who will do that for Judy's dream of an age-integrated village for the twenty-first century?

Perhaps a group of Del Webb's successors?

It's possible. Some of the biggest homebuilders, including a group who have made their reputation focused on age-segregated housing, have started constructing deliberately age-mixed developments. Paying attention to the rise in multigenerational living, as more boomers and their millennial children move in together, Lennar is promoting its NextGen model, which includes space for families and "aging parents, live-in caretakers, post-college grown children and more" under one roof, with "privacy intact." Pardee Homes, another big builder, has launched GenSmart Suite to create homes designed to allow multiple generations to once again live together. Although these efforts are usually discussed in terms of an expanded notion of family, they nonetheless contribute to the creation of multigenerational neighborhoods.

A few gifted inventors are thinking even more creatively. Matthias Hollwich, a New York architect, has dreamed up a project he calls Skyler, "a truly intergenerational skyscraper . . . where we can live fulfilling lives from birth to old age in one building that serves us all life long."

"It has been the easy solution to say, 'old people go here' and young people go somewhere else," Hollwich reflects. "That has been the architectural response to aging for the last hundred years." Skyler would turn that type of segregation on its head. The building would house about a thousand people—including kids, teens, working adults, and individuals over sixty-five—in "pooled apartments that eliminate isolation," along with single-family homes. Skyler residents would have access to shared transportation services, day care centers, a health center and infirmary, and a "business continuation center" for those over sixty-five who are "hardly ready to retire."

Bill Thomas, one of the great social innovators of our time, offers yet another solution. He has launched the Minka project to create what he calls "a new kind of house, a compact, digitally native, modular, panelized house that is both affordable and easy to live in." Some might call them tiny homes. Thomas, following Goldilocks's example, says they're "just right" homes for young people starting out and older ones digging in.

It will be interesting to follow the progress of these inventors—not just to see how Treehouse, Skyler, and Minka evolve but to see how these radical ideas inspire and influence others. By shaking things up, perhaps they'll succeed in creating new norms for intergenerational living.

THE INTEGRATORS

Integrators are dreamers and schemers, too, but their goal isn't to upend. It's to blend, bringing together existing age-segregated institutions in ways that create age-integrated ones. Judson Manor, a senior living facility in Cleveland, is one such example.

Staring at Judson Manor's elegant structure, one half expects Barbara Stanwyck to come gliding out the front door. A magnificent former luxury hotel near the Cleveland Clinic, Case Western Reserve University, and many of the city's museums and arts institutions, Judson Manor now houses about 120 older men and women, with an average age of seventy-nine—and seven graduate students.

If Treehouse and Hope Meadows are intentional multigenerational communities, Judson Manor's intergenerational collaboration with the Cleveland Institute of Music is a somewhat serendipitous one.

Back in 2010, residents of Judson Manor realized that the goal of enlivening the cultural life of the retirement community and the need to provide affordable housing for nearby graduate music students might be simultaneously solved. It turned out to be an inspired insight and soon became an artist-in-residence program. In return for free rent in a beautiful building blocks from the Institute of Music, graduate students agree to play music for the residents and participate in meals and other community events.

No surprise, given the setting, that Judson draws retired faculty, physicians, medical researchers, and other well-educated (and often well-heeled) individuals wanting to be in an area teeming with intellectual activity and culture. Yet in years past, an invisible gulf remained between Judson and the surrounding institutions filled with young people. That changed when a partnership introduced the power of proximity and brought older and younger people who had something in common—a love of music, art, and learning—next door to one another.

Initially there were concerns about wild parties and out-of-place young people, worries that dissipated quickly when the joint committee of Judson staff and residents reviewed the applications. Students had to write an essay about why they wanted to live at Judson Manor; free rent alone was a nonstarter. Although a couple of students haven't worked out, the program has been a success in ways extending well beyond the concerts and classes originally envisioned.

The stories are often touching. A former artist in residence, Caitlin Lynch forged a close relationship with her neighbor, Clara Catliota—so close, in fact, that the young woman asked Catliota to be the flower girl at her wedding in Oregon. The ninety-something woman couldn't make the trip but instead threw a second wedding party for the couple at Judson.

Another resident, Laura Berick, met violin student and artist in residence Tiffany Tieu when she was walking her poodle, Charlie. She asked Tiffany if she liked dogs. She did. Soon Tiffany was picking up spending money as Laura's dog walker, while the two formed a kind of amalgam between a grandparent-grandchild relationship and a close friendship built on their mutual interest in the arts, cooking, stylish shoes, and, of course, man's best friend.

The relationship has changed Tieu's views about aging. "Laura to me is like a grandma and also a friend and a confidant," she says. "We cook and sit around and talk about our problems and things that concern us. In a way it is almost like being in a college dorm. . . . There are so many people here from different places, from different backgrounds. It *might* be a little bit quieter than a normal college dorm," she acknowledges, "but I think we still have just as much fun."

Tiffany graduated and became assistant concertmaster at the Municipal de Santiago, Ópera Nacional de Chile, but the two women remain in close touch. Not long ago, Tiffany rescued a dog on the streets of Santiago and named it Charlie, after Laura's poodle.

Judson residents reach out to students younger than Tiffany, as well. Many older residents volunteer at the Intergenerational School, a nearby K–8 public charter school dedicated to creating a multigenerational community. Founders Peter and Cathy Whitehouse bring young and old together in many ways, but they also bring together young and younger. Cathy Whitehouse's ideal: the one-room schoolhouse reborn, where children of three- or four-year age spans learn together, advancing not by age but by mastery. It's working. The Inter-generational School emphasizes caring, connection, and character; refuses to "cream" (admit only the most gifted students) or prepare kids slavishly for standardized tests; and often outperforms not only almost all other schools in Cleveland but schools throughout Ohio.

It says something about the resonance of the Judson experiment that when I arrived to see the program firsthand, I intersected with a contingent of visiting Swedish academics and social policy experts. Scandinavian policy experts making a pilgrimage to Cleveland for insights and inspiration about enlightened social innovation? Sounds far-fetched, but the scholars from Mid Sweden University described confronting the same issues we face with age segregation and its dele-terious consequences. They were looking for solutions.

The Judson idea, although unique in many ways, has a growing number of incarnations around the world. At the Humanitas long-term care facility in Deventer, in the Netherlands, a half-dozen students are living rent-free in return for thirty hours of volunteer work per month. The program has spread to other nursing homes in the Netherlands and been adapted in Lyon, France. Helsinki has its own model, although instead of university students doing tasks for their keep, the young people's main job is simply to interact with the residents.

Here in the United States, two young innovators—Noelle Marcus and Rachel Goor—have created Nesterly, a higher-tech way to con-nect older people with extra room in their houses with young people, graduate students in particular, who need manageable rent and are willing to perform chores in return for reduced costs. They are inven-tors and integrators all at once.

The starting point for the two women was conquering the affordable-housing challenge in so many major cities, particularly for young people starting out and struggling to make ends meet. Marcus had gone to graduate school from a job in New York City govern-ment, where she'd focused on economic development and housing. In doing research for a paper, she discovered that by 2035, one of three households (some 49.6 million overall) will be led by a person over sixty-five, and 48 percent of these individuals will be living alone. At the same time, Marcus and Goor were aware, from research and their own efforts to find affordable housing in the Boston area, that there was a potential fit between supply and demand.

When I talked with Marcus and Goor, who met in their first year at MIT in 2015, they said that connecting supply and demand was just the beginning. Both were inspired by Maggie Kuhn. They were close to their own grandmothers, too, and felt an emotional connection to (and a passion for) the issue of intergenerational living. Marcus describes age segregation as the last great divide after racial and class segregation in housing.

The women hope to enable matches that cross all three barriers—race, age, and class—bringing together millennial students from very different backgrounds with their boomer hosts. In Marcus's words, "Everyone wants meaning in their lives, and building these kinds of relationships can create a lot of meaning."

Today, Nesterly is in its second year, located in the Robin Hood Foundation's Blue Ridge Labs in Brooklyn. It has won a string of awards for social innovators, including the MIT Global Ideas Challenge and New York City's Big Apps contest.

Although Nesterly piloted a small number of Boston-area matches in its first year, the company has over one thousand users on its site in the second—and big future plans. Marcus and Goor hope to add undergraduates to the mix and expand to the many other markets where student housing is scarce and the number of older people with spare rooms is abundant.

Gorham House—a retirement and assisted-living facility built around a preschool outside Portland, Maine—is both kindred spirit and contrast to Judson Manor. Whereas the former connects older people and college students, the latter brings together senior living and early childhood education.

Coming up the driveway leading to Gorham House, I was struck by the bright colors of the children's playground and its location—right next to the main entrance. Then there were the sounds of laughter, mostly children's laughter, with occasional peals from adults. And I watched as older people gathered, not only on the playground but on their porches overlooking the area. Apparently at Gorham House, the most coveted rooms are the ones nearest the children's playground.

To the right of the main entrance is the sign for and entrance to Gorham House's preschool.

Just as the early childhood program is physically central, it's a central part of how Gorham House presents itself. The facility's website proclaims to parents that their preschool has a competitive advantage over other options: a built-in army of surrogate grandparents, bastions of caring and love, waiting to do their thing. During my visit, I saw children and older people involved in activities like creating art, reading, and playing games—in other words, what you might expect to see when grandparents visit with their own grandchildren.

The benefits are, of course, two-way. The preschool, its website notes, provides "the elderly residents, our 'Grand Friends,' . . . the ability to witness a celebration of life that young children present so well."

Gorham House was created by Bill Gillis, a visionary developer who created a trio of similar facilities in Maine. You could call him a small-scale Del Webb of intergenerational interdependence. Sadly, Gillis passed away a few months before I arrived in Gorham. I would have loved to know what inspired him to move in this direction and blend these previously isolated institutions.

Driving away that day, I couldn't help but think of the contrast between Gorham House and the drab facility where my father was spending his later years in the exclusive presence of frail older people, the antiseptic quiet punctuated not by peals of laughter but only by occasional yells of loneliness or pain. And I couldn't help but wonder why I was unable to find a place like Gorham House for him, someone who would have been so happy to join that army of caring grandparents eager to ply their skills and love.

According to Google Maps, there are 1,590 miles between Gorham, Maine, and Miami's Little Havana district, a journey of twenty-three hours and forty-seven minutes by car, taking the speedy route. The cultural contrast is about as dramatic as the geographic divide—or the difference in temperature in the middle of the winter.

Yet Little Havana's Rainbow Intergenerational Learning Center and Child Care offers a variation on the Gorham House theme, integrating a senior facility with one for little kids. Rainbow is part of—and housed with—the Little Havana Activities and Nutrition Centers of Dade County, which provides comprehensive services to hundreds of isolated and low-income elders in the South Florida area.

But in addition to mingling older adults and kids, Rainbow goes a step beyond. It hires the older people as staff and then helps them receive additional training to become certified early childhood educators—in some cases, to get higher education degrees in the field.

Annie Benedetti runs the program today. Her staffers come primarily from two groups—low-income neighborhood residents (mostly from Cuba), trying to get a leg up, and refugees, many of them professionals (from Venezuela, Peru, and elsewhere), determined to find their footing in a new land. All must learn English and earn their certification to work with the children.

Benedetti didn't start the Rainbow program, and it wasn't born out of a desire to end age segregation. Decades earlier, grandparents from the neighborhood would arrive at the senior facility for meals, with their grandchildren in tow. Because federal guidelines prohibited providing lunch for anyone but the low-income seniors, the Little Havana Activities Center leadership was faced with a problem—what to do with the kids. They solved it by creating the childcare center; then, adpating the natural pattern in many intergenerational Latino households, they employed the older population coming to the center as workers there.

Over time, the center's reach has grown well beyond the grand-children of those using senior services at the Little Havana Activities Center. And the center has gone from a simple day care for the kids to an accredited early childhood education program, in both Little Havana and Miami Beach, built around high standards for the older adults who work there four to five hours a day. That's been a high priority of Benedetti's. "These are professionals teaching children," she says, not babysitters.

Rainbow offers a glimpse of the power of colocating institutions, where genuine relationships are formed between older and younger people, and of a potential solution to much of America's burgeoning childcare workforce woes. Why not train a corps of grandparent-age women and men to become early childhood professionals?

The idea of colocating senior centers and nursing homes with early childhood programs has been steadily gaining ground over the past two decades. Generations United, an organization that was created nearly thirty years ago to improve the lives of children, youth, and older adults through intergenerational collaboration, is the undis-puted authority on these colocation efforts. In June 2018, Generations United and the Ohio State University released a report documenting 105 "shared sites" in the United States that pair youth and elders in the same physical location, with activities that bring the two groups together.

"The signs point to shared sites as an approach primed for the limelight," the report states. "Greater awareness of their potential will not only break down the barriers of age segregation but will forge long-lasting and life-changing intergenerational bonds."

Generations United's CEO Donna Butts says these sites also attack loneliness among the elderly, which is fast becoming a debilitating and costly health issue. Research from the University of California, San Francisco shows that nearly half of adults over sixty-five (43 percent) feel lonely, and AARP researchers connect isolation among older adults with increased health-care costs—nearly $7 billion in additional Medicare spending every year.

THE INFILTRATORS

Infiltrators, in my view, are the innovators finding new ways to insinuate older or younger individuals into previously age-segregated settings, in the process integrating these institutions.

The movie *The Intern* provides a great example. In it, Robert De Niro plays a seventy-year-old widower searching for purpose. Eager to get out of the house, he takes a job as a "senior intern" at an online fashion start-up, earning the trust of the young CEO (played by Anne Hathaway), providing sound business advice, and becoming a real mentor to her and other young colleagues.

The movie could have been based on the Encore Fellowships program, an example of how to infiltrate the workplace with a new source of experienced talent that tips the scale toward age-integration. Encore Fellowships insert seasoned professionals like De Niro's character in high-impact, paid assignments in the social sector. The idea is to give those finishing up their midlife careers the opportunity to spend six to twelve months at a nonprofit, learning and contributing their skills and knowledge to a cause.

It's a two-way exchange. The Encore Fellow gets a much-needed bridge from a midlife career to a potential encore, and the nonprofit gets the benefit of skills honed for decades in corporate life, plus a taste of the value of a multigenerational workforce. Often, the fellow actually does mentor the CEO, as in the movie.

Such was the case with James Otieno. James retired from his job as a vice president of executive services and compensation at Hewlett Packard. When offered the chance to be one of the first group of Encore Fellows in 2009, he jumped, signing on to help the Silicon Valley Education Foundation with human resources, finance and board governance, and eventually overall organizational strategy.

He earned $25,000 for his efforts, and at the end of his fellowship, then-CEO Muhammed Chaudhry offered him a job as vice president of partnerships, strategy, and technology. Otieno "walks on water," a grateful Chaudhry told the *Mercury News*.

James, an immigrant from Kenya who believes that education is the key to success in life, accepted and stayed for years. Today he's juggling board positions for other education-centered organizations and working on entrepreneurial efforts to build schools and spur economic development in his native continent.

In the past eight years, nearly two thousand Encore Fellows have been matched with assignments in close to fifty metropolitan areas. Companies—including Qualcomm, Cisco, Hewlett Packard, IBM, and Intel—have sponsored Encore Fellows, who have bridged sectors, race, and age. They've advised many a nonprofit CEO. And they've contributed nearly two million hours of service and an estimated $200 million in talent to organizations fighting for a better future.

The program not only provides older people with a line on their résumé and credibility in a new sector but offers them an opportunity to reset priorities and turn their attention to both learning and mentoring.

While Encore Fellows are infiltrating social-sector workplaces, others in search of a midlife reset are beginning to infiltrate college classrooms—an innovation long overdue.

With fifty- or sixty-year working lives becoming the norm, it doesn't make much sense to confine college to our teens and twenties. Universities are beginning, slowly, to agree. Among those leading the way is the University of Minnesota Advanced Careers (UMAC) program for boomers transitioning from midlife careers to encores. Some call it a gap year for grown-ups, between the end of one chapter and the start of whatever's next.

Following pioneering models at Harvard and Stanford, the University of Minnesota recently launched a more modestly priced two-semester program designed to help those ending midlife careers discover and prepare for encore careers or volunteer work in the social sector. As a result, all three universities have witnessed older and younger adults coming together as peers.

I saw this firsthand while teaching a social-entrepreneurship class at Stanford in 2017. Nearly half the students were fifty-, sixty-, and seventy-year-olds in Stanford's Distinguished Careers Institute, and the rest were undergraduate and graduate students. The older and younger individuals worked together on projects. There was obvious synergy.

That natural flow was a surprise to some of the younger students in the University of Minnesota class on "The Future of Work and Life in the 21st Century," also including UMAC fellows.

"The first time I walked into the class, I was like, 'Why are there a bunch of old people in here with us?'" Madison Smiley, twenty, told a reporter from the *Wall Street Journal*. "I was afraid it was going to feel like taking a class with my mom."

Smiley saw the benefits soon enough. "My peers aren't in the workforce," she said. The older students "were able to share the problems they have actually seen." By the end of the class, the students took group photographs. Professor Phyllis Moen, UMAC's founder and one of the first academics to study the new stage of life beyond midlife, says it's the first time that has happened in her forty-plus years in higher education.

Leaders of all three university programs have told me that as older students engage in projects with twenty-something undergraduates, they end up mentoring the younger students. And the learning is reciprocal. It's not hard to imagine a rethinking of the arc of higher education in America that would make this type of age-integration and interaction the norm.

Today wide-ranging efforts to create a university for all ages are taking place at an array of institutions in the United States and across the globe, from the University of Rhode Island to Dublin City College in Ireland to Washington University in St. Louis, where noted gerontology scholar (and Experience Corps researcher) Nancy

Morrow-Howell has drafted an effort to bring older people into every aspect of the university. Morrow-Howell would like to promote classes to all ages and add new ones that would appeal to older students, engage older adults in the planning of research on productive aging, connect university retirees to campus life, age-integrate housing, dedicate physical space for older people on campus, and more. Her goal is nothing less than to build "the first comprehensive age-integrated research university in the world."

To be sure, inventing, integrating, and infiltrating are just three ways to move from accepting age apartheid to embracing our increasingly multigenerational world. There are undoubtedly other approaches to moving from the present reality to a better one. They may not even begin with the letter *i*! But the imperative is the same: we need more social innovation to make the most of these possibilities.

PUMPING UP THE VOLUME

Every year for the past decade, the World Economic Forum has organized a summer meeting. Unlike the "Winter Davos" held at Davos in Switzerland, the "Summer Davos" is convened in China. The formal name is the Annual Meeting of New Champions, the defining theme is innovation, and the participants are all heralded as disrupters of the status quo. In 2014, I was invited as a Social Entrepreneur of the Year.

In truth, there were a couple dozen Social Entrepreneurs of the Year, but I was honored and grateful nonetheless. When I began mingling, though, I had a sinking feeling, one I'd experienced often at other gatherings highlighting innovation—a sense of being alone. There was no one else there working to engage the talent and experience of older people or, for that matter, to bring this group together with young people.

This was all the more striking because the World Economic Forum's leader, Klaus Schwab, was himself nearing eighty, at the height of his creativity and just about to come out with a new book about the coming trends reshaping society. We were in China, which is projected to have more older people by midcentury than the total US population. And, to add insult to injury, there was no lack of interest in longer lives. The gathering was awash in immortalists proclaiming break-throughs in technology and medicine aimed at dramatically extend-ing life and health.

There are advantages to being a token representative of an issue; the novelty value probably makes it easier to get selected for honors like this one. But, all organizational modesty aside, Encore.org alone isn't going to get us to the promised land.

I came away from the Summer Davos convinced that we needed to pump up the volume on innovation. Since then, at Encore we have scraped together enough money to make small investments in social innovators of all ages with creative ideas for bringing the generations together. In our first year, with little fanfare, we got nearly two hun-dred applicants for the Gen2Gen Encore Prize. Most were grassroots leaders drawing inspiration from their own experiences and starting organizations to extend them into the wider community.

Nominees included Pushy Moms, a group of older mothers who helped their own kids apply to and graduate from college and are now using that experience to help largely first-generation students at LaGuardia Community College in New York apply for four-year degrees. And Grandmas2Go, a group that trains older people as coaches to help support struggling new parents. And Hire Autism, an organization that's recruiting older mentors—perhaps parents or grandparents of children with autism—to help coach young people with autism who have graduated from high school but are struggling to find jobs. And, as we're seeing in our second year with the Encore Prize, there are many more great ideas out there—hundreds, perhaps thousands.

I have to believe that Maggie Kuhn would be thrilled with all this dreaming and scheming, but I know we have a long way to go and many innovations to see before we achieve true age-integration in our daily lives.

Will these innovations—small beacons for our multigenerational society—manage to break through and inspire a wider rethinking of the way we live, learn, and work? Will they grow as powerful and widespread as the age-segregating innovations of the past one hundred years? Will they be able to influence the broader culture in similar ways, but by bringing us together rather than pulling us apart?

It's not easy to change culture and institutions. It took a powerful wave of change to separate people by age, and it will take an equally forceful and imaginative counterwave to bring people together again.

There is some irony that we have to do this in the first place. Bill Thomas, who has done so much to humanize nursing homes and now is working through the Minka project to create affordable multigenerational communities, puts it this way: "We live in a culture, time, and place where creative people have to use creative means to accomplish something that was always the most ordinary, customary thing in the human experience: older people and younger people sharing their lives."

To that I can only say, amen.

Chapter 6
A VILLAGE FOR ALL AGES

Sister Geraldine Tan, an energetic woman in her sixties, speaks rapidly and is given to sweeping gestures. She wears the abundant, flowing white robes of the Canossian Daughters of Charity, and they threaten to engulf her small frame. But Sister Geraldine—who trained in the hospice movement in the UK and is now the executive director of the St. Joseph's Home for the Aged and Hospice in Singapore—is not easily overwhelmed.

St. Joseph's is not your typical nursing home. It's architecturally striking, with tropical flora, open pavilions, and airy rooms. Natural light and trade winds flow through its floors. It's large, accommodating some four hundred older people.

And the people it serves aren't all elderly. The facility includes a childcare center for about fifty children, ages two months to six years. At the center of St. Joseph's courtyard is the nation's first intergenerational playground, designed to leverage the power of proximity and encourage natural interaction between the older people living at the facility and the little ones in the childcare center.

The neighborhood isn't typical either. St. Joseph's is located in Jurong West, an industrial area that's gone high tech. Google Singapore is next door. On the other side of St. Joseph's is the Boys' Home, housing young people who have been in trouble with the authorities. Across the street is a primary school. The massive Supply Chain City building—a "state-of-the-art facility that serves as Asia's supply chain nerve centre"—is less than a hundred yards away. St. Joseph's sits in the middle of it all, a bastion of humanity.

Even with strong cultural values regarding respect for elders, Singapore's leaders see the generations growing apart. They are eager to bring them back together, to find new ways to do old things.

That fits Sister Geraldine's vision. She is determined to create an environment that encompasses the full "circle of life"—with children at its center. "They remind us of the purpose of life and of the importance of play and simplicity," she says, describing the approach as her "full circle" model. "There is birth and there is death," says Sister Geraldine. "At both ends, we all need someone to tend to us."

In keeping, the childcare center aims to foster bonds that benefit young and old. Students at the primary school across the street visit regularly and are mentored by the seniors. Boys' Home residents operate a coffee cart in the central courtyard, delivering drinks to the older residents at St. Joseph's, another way Sister Geraldine is hoping to instigate meaningful relationships that cross the generations. Someday, perhaps the young Googlers next door will find a reason to stop by.

Even that won't be enough for Sister Geraldine. In Singapore, as in some other Asian societies, death is often treated as a taboo subject. Children and younger generations are shielded from the reality of life's end, and if someone dies at home, the property's value can plummet.

Sister Geraldine wants to change that, too, by creating a sense of the wholeness of life, pulling mortality into the open, targeting the fear of aging and death. To that end, she joined forces with a prominent philanthropist in Singapore to create a project called Happy Coffins. Its goal: "to overturn the stigma of death by transforming the coffin from a symbol of fear, grief, and dread into a celebration of life, love, and hope."

The project engaged artists from around the globe to create three coffin designs expressing the life, spirit, and desired legacy of older St. Joseph's residents. Happy Coffins creates "respectfully 'out-of-the-box' interpretations of that final 'in-the-box' journey," the promotional materials explain.

AROUND THE WORLD

I arrived for my tour of St. Joseph's not long after getting off an eighteen-hour plane ride from San Francisco (talk about an in-the-box journey), in sweltering Southeast Asian heat and with a time zone difference flipping day and night. It was the first leg of a weeklong around-the-world tour—Singapore, London, then home for a two-day collapse—in search of insights and understanding from abroad on how we might bring the generations together.

I hoped the trip would shed light on two global developments with potential to advance the generativity revolution. I would go to London to understand the power of a pied piper, in the form of renowned *Financial Times* journalist Lucy Kellaway and her effort to call forth the over-fifty population to improve the lives of the next generation. Could a single prominent innovator, Kellaway, inspire throngs of people over fifty to become teachers and, in the process, change how many more seek purpose and legacy in the years beyond midlife?

And I went to Singapore to understand the opposite approach. Instead of a charismatic individual catalyst, Singapore offered a grand national plan to invest $3 billion in Singapore dollars ($2.1 billion in US dollars) and become the envy of the world's aging societies. That's a staggering investment, even if spread out over a period of years. I wanted to know if Singapore could really create a comprehensive scheme to make the most of an aging population, marshal massive amounts of public and private resources to enable olders to support youngers, and recreate a village that works for all ages. Or was it all just hype?

Singapore is an island city-state with a population of just under four million permanent residents, about the size of Chicago. Like much of Asia, Singapore is aging fast. It's also one of the most diverse places on earth (and one of the best for eating, not an unrelated attribute).

"Aging is really the single most important demographic shift that will affect the future of Singapore," Dr. Amy Khor, the government's senior minister of state for health, says. It's a fair point. In 1970, one in thirty-one Singaporeans was sixty-five or older. The number today: one in eight. By 2030 it will be one in four. That's a doubling, from about 440,000 people over sixty-five today to more than 900,000 by 2030. As in much of the world, the change is caused by both increasing longevity and decreasing birth rates.

So what's in the grand plan? In February of 2016, Khor announced the Action Plan for Successful Ageing, an ambitious collection of some seventy initiatives covering a wide array of issues—health, learning, volunteerism, employment, housing, transportation, public spaces, social inclusion, health care, protection for vulnerable elders, research, and more. A leitmotif throughout is engaging older people to support the next generation.

Singapore's leaders thought of everything—and funded it. To bring the generations together, they're launching initiatives to help older people retool for second acts, to recruit young people to teach technology and social media skills to older people, and to help community organizations better use older volunteers. They're promoting "3Gen flats" to help older people, younger people, and those in the middle live in close proximity. In one of the grand plan's most striking features, they're creating a "Kampong for All Ages." "Kampong" is the Malay word for village, and the plan envisions a future Singapore built around a cherished element of the past, the multigenerational village.

How will Singapore create the spirit of a village in a very modern city? With colocated eldercare and childcare facilities, to start. And, to spur new thinking, the grand plan includes a $200 million ($140 million in US dollars) National Innovation Challenge, which will include research on promising models, plus incentives to inspire fresh ideas for making the most of the multigenerational society.

I sat down with two young architects at the powerful CDB, the ministry that oversees all land use and development in the peninsular country, where space is at an absolute premium. They showed me plans for the Admiralty Kampong, a new mixed-use development in a suburban neighborhood built from the ground up to encourage connection between the generations. The complex will include a ground-floor plaza with a grocery store and eateries. There's a day care center, along with assisted-living services, a day center for elders with more extensive needs, and lots of opportunities and incentives for socializing.

The idea is to use community design to recreate natural opportunities for cross-generational support, to move beyond program to proximity. This extensive and conscious effort to bring the generations together is all the more striking in an Asian society where this kind of interaction and care between young and old, especially within families, happened naturally for much of Singapore's history. Now in the context of the fast-paced, highly mobile, and globally oriented twenty-first-century society, there's a need to find new ways to do these time-honored things.

THE CIRCLE OF LIFE

I admit being taken with the advertised features of Singapore's grand plan, but my burning question upon arrival and throughout my visit was, is it real or a mirage?

Some experiences were underwhelming. At one point, I visited the oldest center in the country attempting to bring children, adolescents, and older adults together. The diversity of the program, like the diversity of Singapore, was impressive, mixing many different ethnic backgrounds, as well as ages. Yet the contact between generations was mostly superficial—the patina of proximity without much in the way of meaningful relationships and genuine interaction.

But those encounters were the exception. For the most part, I witnessed a sense of common purpose to realize the plan's goals, which felt as much about leadership and a shared vision than even the vast sums being spent—although I can't quite get over my envy of the money.

Two lessons in particular stood out for me. First, not having much land can be a powerful impetus for change. Scarcity of space might have bred conflict but instead is prompting creative thinking about combining institutional purposes to wring the most social value out of limited square footage. Second, I found the instinct to combine old and new (that new-way-to-do-old-things approach) everywhere, the same progressive nostalgia animating so many of the American schemes I've encountered.

On my final day, I visited a church initiative that stood as a kind of faith-based bookend with the St. Joseph's experience that started my trip. St. John's-St. Margaret's is a well-established Anglican congregation in the leafy Dover neighborhood near the National University of Singapore. The church is in the midst of creating a large senior living facility and early childhood center. When completed, with tens of millions of dollars raised by the church from private sources, the project may be even more impressive than St. Joseph's intergenerational campus.

Breaking ground in the summer of 2017, the design and planning were four years in the making, prompted by the expiration of the church's lease on its government-owned land. To stay on its prized plot in a desirable location, St. John's-St. Margaret's was required to "intensify" the use of the land—in other words, to do more social good with the space. The congregation decided not only to build a nursing home and senior programming as originally intended but to find ways to simultaneously support young children. I love the notion of *intensifying* the land—another way of saying every dollar spent (at least) twice.

For insights, the St. John's-St. Margaret's team headed to the United States, visiting facilities here that bring the generations together for mutual benefit, including the Providence Mount St. Vincent's Intergenerational Learning Center in Seattle, the subject of a documentary, *The Growing Season*. Indeed, it was striking to see how many of the ideas that Singapore was scaling had roots in the United States or were inspired by US innovations.

Another source of inspiration for the church is a passage from Zechariah 8:4–5, one that describes the renewed city of Jerusalem as a kind of cross-generational paradise. "Old men and old women shall again sit in the streets of Jerusalem, each with staff in hand because of great age. And . . . the city shall be full of boys and girls playing in its streets."

When finished in 2020, the St. John's-St. Margaret's effort will result in a 273-person nursing home facility, a senior center for 100 older people, and an early childhood center, including a kindergarten, for 200 children. The name for the initiative is Project Spring-Winter. Its primary goal: to build meaningful relationships that flow down the generational chain, so older people can experience "purpose and hope as they engage with the young."

When I visited with the congregation members leading this effort, they told me of an unanticipated side benefit. While working on the plans, they realized that the church itself had become highly age segregated, scheduling services and activities that separated people by age—children's services and services for adults, oftentimes held at the same time in separate rooms. Now, prompted by the research that's gone into Project Spring-Winter, they're thinking about how best to age-integrate the congregation.

Sherlyn Lee, one of the Project Spring-Winter leaders and a congregant, told me she hopes the new effort will help restore a sense of the "circle of life" at the church and throughout Singapore. I was struck by the symmetry: Sherlyn and Sister Geraldine had opened and closed my visit with essentially the same phrase.

"We're basically reinventing the original intergenerational concept," Lee told me, describing how old British churches make visitors walk across the flat tombstones as they approach. "It reminds you of your mortality," she said. "We have our baby baptisms here . . . we walk down the same aisle at weddings . . . then you have your funeral in the same place."

COMPREHENSIVE ACTION

As I was flying to London that evening, my mind was still spinning from Singapore's efforts to recapture the Kampong spirit.

The nation's leaders have married common sense and pragmatic approaches with a soaring level of ambition. They've spurred a wide array of investments extending well beyond public dollars and involved more than just public leaders, too—philanthropists, businesspeople, academics, faith leaders, educators, and lots of citizens.

What's happening in Singapore has the potential to transform life for its residents and serve as a model for other nations. I should be thrilled to see something similar happening here in my lifetime, but I confess to mixed emotions. Singapore's efforts are uplifting—yet, when compared to the state of things in the United States, witnessing that kind of national commitment can be a little deflating at the same time.

All the more because we've thought expansively ourselves in the past.

In 1956, a young US senator, John F. Kennedy, talked about the untapped potential of older people, commenting that we were wasting resources of "incalculable value." Once in the White House, he called on young people—those idealistic baby boomers setting out on their journey—to "ask not" what their country could do for them. He created the Peace Corps as one way for them to answer that challenge.

Few remember that Kennedy also articulated ambitious plans for mobilizing older people to serve society, particularly younger generations. His words and plans would be groundbreaking if unveiled today.

On February 21, 1963, some nine months before his assassination, Kennedy stood up before Congress to articulate the challenge invoked at the outset of this book: "It is not enough for a great nation merely to have added new years to life; our objective must also be to add new life to those years." He decried the loneliness and disconnection faced by many over sixty and "the wall of inertia" that needlessly exists between older people and their communities, impoverishing both.

Kennedy's remarks contained lofty rhetoric and memorable lines but went further, laying out plans for "comprehensive action" to stimulate continued productivity and service to society by older people. And Kennedy recommended legislation to establish a new five-year program aimed at making it happen.

Among his prescriptions were employment programs to retrain older people to provide "child care in centers for working mothers," a National Service Corps providing opportunities for older people to serve their communities and young people, and a way for older people to be involved in programs to prevent what was then called "juvenile delinquency."

Indeed, to anchor his point about wasting resources of vast value, Kennedy went on to rattle off the skill levels in the recently retired population of the day, arguing that his proposed National Service Corps would be "an ideal outlet for those whose energy, idealism, and ability did not suddenly end in retirement." What's more, he added, "The Peace Corps, which has no upper age limit, has already drawn upon this reservoir of talent."

It all sounds a lot like what's getting under way in Singapore—something we haven't seen or heard from an American president since. The absence was all the more notable in the 2016 presidential election, when the two nominees and almost all of the contenders were well past sixty yet almost never spoke about "adding life to years," much less calling their age peers to a higher and more enduring purpose.

LONDON CALLING

Predictably, I arrived in London completely exhausted and under the weather. What was I thinking when I booked a round-the-world-in-a-week trip? Still, I was determined to get an early view of Now Teach, which had just put its first small group of teachers in classrooms.

A year earlier, Lucy Kellaway had made a big splash when she announced plans to quit her prestigious perch as one of the *Financial Times*'s most beloved columnists to become a math teacher in a low-income London school.

Committing to the vocational shift was a courageous step, but Kellaway didn't stop there. She challenged her readers "of a certain age" to follow. "I want to hear from anyone who is ready to chuck in the corporate life and come with me," she wrote. "I can't be the only 50-something person in the country to want a second career in this most noble of professions."

Kellaway launched a nonprofit to realize her vision of a corps of older, impassioned teachers eager to help the next generation thrive. With her daughter in Teach First, a program for recent college graduates, Kellaway considered calling her organization Teach Last but got talked out of the title, settling instead on Now Teach. Her goal was nevertheless to flip the Teach First formula, where brilliant young people taught before heading off to "McKinsey/PwC/Goldman," to one where brilliant older people taught after leaving distinguished careers in other sectors.

The response was an outpouring of interest. Eventually more than a thousand people came forward for forty-seven positions. Kellaway was careful to anticipate the myriad ways that things might go wrong. She and her cofounder, millennial and school reform expert Katie Waldegrave, worked with a nonprofit, Ark Teacher Training, to develop a training program explicitly for career changers.

Chris Forsyth, a partner at the prominent international law firm Freshfields and an expert in intellectual property law, was one of those moved to answer Lucy Kellaway's challenge. He'd always fancied himself as a teacher, and the Brexit vote—a failure of education, he says—convinced him of the urgent need to improve schooling in the UK. What's more, his children were off to university, and professionally, practicing corporate law had run its course. It was time.

Selected from the vast applicant pool, Forsyth was placed at Ark Putney Academy in north London. Surrounded by public housing for low- and moderate-income families, Ark Putney's focus is character education for students between the ages of eleven and eighteen, particularly those who have struggled academically or who have been in the care of the state. The school's six pillars—team work, community, enthusiasm, commitment, effort, and independence—are stenciled on the walls at the main entrance.

With gray-black hair and dark-rimmed glasses, wearing an open-collared Oxford shirt, Forsyth looks at home at Ark Putney, but he admits to considerable apprehension before starting. "You'll be useless," Forsyth's own son told him. "The kids will walk all over you."

When we met a few months into the school year, Forsyth was learning on his feet, to be sure, but navigating the new terrain, gaining confidence, and feeling fulfilled. At the end of the first year, he wrote to say how much he had enjoyed the Now Teach experience, that he remained as committed as ever to teaching, and "would recommend it to anyone."

In addition to bringing a wave of talent into the schools, Forsyth and his fellow Now Teach recruits are taking a step toward age-integrating the teaching profession in the UK. Of the thirty-five thousand new teachers in the country in 2016, just one hundred were older than fifty-five. Kellaway, Forsyth, and the other nearly four dozen Now Teach pioneers—most in their fifties and sixties—joined them in September 2017, working in schools with primarily low-income students, covering subjects where significant teacher shortages exist in the UK, most notably science, math, and languages.

The road hasn't been entirely smooth. Several Now Teach recruits have already quit, and others, Kellaway acknowledged, "are wobbling," airing concerns about discipline, stress, student apathy, multitasking, and the "relentless ringing of the bell." Kellaway herself says that "teaching is brutal," leaving her in "a permanent state of agitation."

I missed the chance to meet with Kellaway due to my worsening flu. I had many questions for her. Fortunately, Kellaway has chronicled her own odyssey and that of the inaugural cohort of Now Teach teachers thoroughly in a string of unflinching and insightful columns. Nearing the end of her first semester, she wrote this in the *Financial Times:*

> One of my fellow Now Teach trainees, who in a previous life was a top civil servant, says teaching is a bit like having a baby—it is more shattering, more difficult—but also more rewarding—than anyone can prepare you for. For me, it's like having a baby in a different way.

When my first child was born 26 years ago an unlooked-for bonus was that for the first time in my life I had something more pressing to think about than myself. Becoming a teacher has performed the same miracle professionally—teaching is no longer about me. It's about the students—and more precisely about getting them to learn some maths.

In January 2018, Now Teach announced that it will expand beyond London to Hastings. Recruitment continues with this appeal on Now Teach's homepage: "You've had a successful career. Now do something more important. Now teach."

PARTING QUESTIONS

Finally home and on the mend, my round-the-world odyssey produced a string of realizations and sought-after answers, along with some uncomfortable questions.

Unlike Singapore, we have no grand plan. We don't have billions of dollars to engage older people in ways that solve societal problems, serve future generations, and provide opportunities to live a legacy.

We can't boast a JFK ascending the bully pulpit with an "ask not" speech aimed at the generation the Peace Corps was created for in the first place. We don't have leaders in Congress agitating for these changes.

We can't even claim our own equivalent of Lucy Kellaway, the charismatic innovator and activist dedicating herself to serving the next generation and challenging peers to join her.

Indeed, we've been heading in the opposite direction for decades. Pushing older people to disengage from society, extolling a "golden years" existence built around graying as playing, peddling age-segregated playgrounds animated by what the late feminist icon Betty Friedan once termed the "youth short-circuit."

It's all at odds with the developmental imperatives of older generations, the needs of younger ones, and the requirements of a society that for the first time ever has more of the former than the latter.

Over the past half century, we've made what's natural unnatural—and oftentimes impossible.

So where does that leave us? More to the point: How can we turn things around? How can we realize the promise of a multigenerational future while averting predictions of coming conflict, dysfunction, and despair? And how can we do so in time to ride the wave of demographic change already upon us?

Chapter 7

REROUTING THE RIVER OF LIFE

Near where I live in Berkeley, there is an underground stream that flows down from the hills, winding through the University of California campus, in and around affluent neighborhoods with dramatic views of San Francisco and the Golden Gate Bridge, then through single-story homes in the flatlands before emptying into the bay.

For many years that stream remained largely buried, covered over in an earlier era to enable more efficient building and to prevent children from falling into the water. Then a collection of urban environmental activists and visionary architects formed a group with a radical idea: uncover the stream. To their surprise, city departments fought the idea, unhappy about all the extra work and maintenance a resurgent stream would entail. But the activists prevailed. And the stream, which had been flowing underground for all those years, was once again exposed.

Today Strawberry Creek is one of the great sources of vitality in my city. It's surrounded by flora (and some fauna, including a flock of wild turkeys), walking paths, and all manner of vibrancy.

It reminds me of what we've done to the spirit of generativity over the past half century. We buried it. But deep down, that spirit has always been flowing. And today it is slowly being uncovered and rediscovered.

There's no stream restoration project for the generative spirit. But as the previous chapters have sought to chronicle, we are in the midst of what amounts to a bubbling up of myriad innovations and actions, oftentimes at the grassroots level.

We may have rerouted the river of life decades ago, but these efforts are beginning—fitfully, messily, slowly—to return the flow to its natural course, and to the surface.

This change is not being driven from the top down; it's coming mostly from the bottom up. It's not being spearheaded (yet) by prominent leaders or by soaring schemes; it's being led rather by scrappy entrepreneurs with good ideas about how to engage older people to help support the next generation.

We might not have a grand plan—but we can boast a great ferment.

And it's unfolding despite remarkably little investment or support. We have nothing approximating the innovation fund that's part of the Singapore plan, or for that matter similar investment pools in the UK and elsewhere. The venture capitalists aren't swarming around these ideas as they are around ones aimed at lengthening life spans. Government dollars are hard to find, and we lack anything resembling a significant or coherent policy in this arena. A mere 1 percent of philanthropy goes into anything related to aging, and a tiny fraction of that goes into productive opportunities for engagement across the generations.

Yet, somehow, the stream of creativity persists. It says something that Scandinavians are coming to Cleveland to see the breakthrough ideas under way there and that Singaporeans are going to Seattle, on the trail of insights and inspiration.

For me, one of the most encouraging developments is that more and more of this innovation is being spearheaded by young people, upstart social entrepreneurs who blend fresh approaches with an appreciation of the unique value of elders. Individuals like Catalina Garcia, who founded Gma Village to connect low-income parents who need part-time or odd-hour childcare with surrogate grandmas, and Nesterly cofounders Noelle Marcus and Rachel Goor, as well as a new generation of leading architects like Matthias Hollwich.

And there are heartening exceptions among established institutions, as well. AARP, frequently associated in the public mind with the fight to save Social Security and Medicare (not to mention member discounts), is doing much to disrupt the shackles of ageism and outmoded notions of the capacities of older people. I've witnessed this firsthand, as AARP, led by CEO Jo Ann Jenkins, embraced—and adopted—our Experience Corps and Purpose Prize projects, determined to keep these innovations going and expand their impact.

The Eisner Foundation, started by former Disney CEO Michael Eisner and his family, has emerged as a model for philanthropy, becoming the first American foundation to fully dedicate itself to bringing the generations together for mutual benefit. It has also created the Eisner Prize to recognize and invest in groups like Generations United, Experience Corps, the Intergenerational School in Cleveland, the Intergenerational Center at Temple University, and Bridge Meadows, a stunning program that has adapted the Hope Meadows model in and around Portland, Oregon.

Taken together, all these developments provide a glimpse of what's possible. I often think of what could happen with much more investment from private sources, government, or philanthropy.

And progress is not just visible in the creative start-ups upending institutional practices. It's exemplified by individuals like Aggie Bennett and Louise Casey on the pediatrics ward of Maine Medical Center, reminding us that we don't have a single person to waste. And by Martha Jones at Taylor Elementary School in Philadelphia, hanging up her coat while "two little arms" wrap around her, demonstrating that the need to be needed is one of the keys to living a meaningful life. And by the wedding party at Judson Manor, where the young newlywed violists are being toasted by their ninety-something neighbor, showing that where there's proximity, relationships across the generations so often bloom.

I see the potential of our multigenerational future when my wife, Leslie, has to rush our ten-year-old son with a 104-degree fever to urgent care and she calls our older neighbor Joyce to come by to hold down the fort. Or when our twelve-year-old wanders over to see Joyce's husband, Jake, to learn how to open the safe where he's accidentally locked all his birthday money—and then lost the key.

These are all examples of practical support interwoven with genuine connection. They add up to ingenuity and resilience in the face of demographic change, an incipient impulse that I like to think of—in true '60s generation terms—as a twenty-first-century back-to-nature movement. Only this time it's back to human nature, and maybe, just maybe, it can help save us from the potential problems of a more-old-than-young society while realizing the vast opportunity this new world presents.

FORGING AHEAD

This book started out with a set of questions: How can we tap the largely underused talent of the older population to support the next generation, not through succumbing to nostalgia but in ways that fit contemporary realities? How can we do so within families but likewise across them and into the broader community? How might we adapt the grandmother hypothesis to the modern-family world?

After all these years of asking and observing, of advocating and innovating, there are a few lessons that stand out. I believe they offer keys to cultural transformation, to institutional reinvention, and to the understanding of why this all matters so much right now.

It's time to go with the flow.

If biology flows downhill, so must culture and society. We need to encourage and uphold roles for older people that align with the developmental imperatives of this period and the natural impulse to generativity.

For one, flowing downhill is a whole lot easier than swimming upstream.

What's more, it's hardly something new. The stream has been flowing since the beginning of time. The word "mentor" comes from Mentor, a wise, older character in *The Odyssey* to whom Odysseus entrusts the care of his son, Telemachus, as the father goes off to war.

Rabbi Lord Jonathan Sacks, the former chief rabbi of the United Kingdom, depicts Moses in this mold, as an older person dedicated to nurturing the next generation. Moses lived to 120 but didn't reach the Promised Land. He invested in a future that he would not actually see but was deeply connected to nonetheless.

"There is something moving about seeing Moses, at almost 120," Sacks writes, "looking forward as well as back, sharing his wisdom with the young, teaching us that while the body may age, the spirit can stay young *ad meah ve-esrim,* until a hundred and twenty, if we keep our ideals, give back to the community, and share our wisdom with those who will come after us, inspiring them to continue what we could not complete."

And if the generative ideal is timeless, it could hardly be timelier for our world of modern families, widespread childlessness, geographic mobility, and new definitions of kinship. My colleague, Marci Alboher, who is in her fifties, wrote recently in the *New York Times* about how people without children, like herself, create a legacy. "I'm lucky to have close relationships with my nephew and other young children in my circle, yet my nurturing instinct kicks into overdrive with people hitting their twenties and starting their careers. I think often about Gloria Steinem, who has had various young women living in her guest room for periods. I yearn for my version of that."

Marci goes on to describe filling her need to be generative by collecting "younger friends with a vengeance" and volunteering with a nonprofit, Girls Write Now. And she quotes Ruth Ann Harnisch, with no biological children, who says, "Even though I've never been pregnant or adopted, it's not in my soul that I have no children. Everybody's child is everybody's child. And I feel responsible for all kids as a resident of this planet."

From Mentor and Moses to Marci.

We have the human beings to do the things that only human beings can do.

In his book *No Easy Victories,* written in the late 1960s, John Gardner projected serious shortages in the caring professions. He argued that these roles would never be automated because they were deeply rooted in human interaction. Older people, he observed, were exceptionally well suited to filling these roles and this void.

Since then an accumulation of research has reinforced Gardner's insights, showing that critically important human abilities—interacting with others, regulating emotions, mediating disputes—peak in later life. What's more, the rise of artificial intelligence and the increased capacity of technology have only underscored the unique importance of humans in performing those tasks that machines cannot match.

Thomas Friedman makes this case in his *New York Times* column "From Hands to Heads to Hearts." He quotes management expert Dov Seidman, who argues that the industrial economy "was about hired hands" and that the knowledge economy "was about hired heads. Now, Seidman says, the "technology revolution is thrusting us into 'the human', which will be more about creating value with hired hearts—all the attributes that can't be programmed into software, like passion, character and collaborative spirit."

The central contribution in the economy and society of the twenty-first century, Seidman adds, will be the thing that machines can never contribute: "deep relationships of trust"—in other words, "a heart."

A little over a month later, Bill Gates, sixty-one at the time, proposed a tax on robots that could be used to pay for empathy work, observing that liberating humans from some kinds of labor would, if done wisely, "let us do a better job of reaching out to the elderly, having smaller class sizes, helping kids with special needs. You know, all of those are things where human empathy and understanding are still very, very unique. And we still deal with an immense shortage of people to help out there."

My journey over the past three decades convinces me that there is no shortage of people to do this work. We're witnessing a population explosion of just the folks who can produce uniquely human things, and many have the longevity and health to do them over a sustained period of time.

It's ironic, isn't it? Technology was supposed to render the skills of older people obsolete, but it may be doing exactly the opposite.

We must age-integrate everything.

We've gotten ourselves stuck in age-segregated communities, schools, and workplaces that drive a wedge between young and old, making it too difficult for the generations to intersect and connect. These arrangements are failing us, and they need to be revamped around both integration and proximity.

I've seen how the power of proximity creates the opportunity for old and young to form and maintain natural bonds. Joyce and Jake are surrogate grandparents to my kids because they live a few doors down. At Judson Manor, Laura Berick, eighty-something, and the twenty-something Tiffany Tieu lived in the same building, often sitting at Laura's dining room table and talking about dogs and shoes. Susan Richards, a boomer, rented space to Harvard postdoc Ayush Rawarnde through Nesterly. Rawarnde helped with chores; Richards found him an afterschool program where he could volunteer. They developed a powerful bond in the process.

We're going to need a lot more proximity. We'll need more Nesterlys "redefining home across generations," as the group says on its website. More senior living facilities and preschools opening next door to one another, as they did at Gorham House. More Intergenerational Schools, more Experience Corps members, more old and young in college classrooms together, and more teachers in their encore careers.

On the job, as we face fifty- or sixty-year careers, we'll have four or five generations working together at the same time. That's a lot of proximity! We'll need more retraining and reskilling, more two-way mentoring programs, more opportunities for the young to become leaders, and more chances for older colleagues to coach them.

The human rights lawyer and activist Bryan Stevenson makes an especially compelling case for proximity's power as a key to social progress in our increasingly divided society. Stevenson adds three other ingredients to his agenda for change—the need to change narratives, to remain hopeful, and to accept a certain degree of discomfort.

I agree with Stevenson on all counts. Breaking down the walls of inertia, crossing divides not just of age but also of race and class, will bring necessary discomfort. At the same time, it will offer a way to reweave the social fabric of today's multigenerational and multicultural society and tomorrow's. And with that, it will bring genuine hope.

In this future, we'll also need to intensify the human assets at our disposal and spend every dollar twice. The way immigrant older women at Rainbow Intergenerational's preschool in Little Havana do by teaching toddlers while retraining for second acts as early childhood educators, and the way Encore Fellows do by helping nonprofits create strategic plans while reskilling for encore careers in the social sector.

This is about a means and an end.

We now know that engaging olders to support youngers, to connect with them in meaningful ways, is one of the routes to well-being in later life. An extensive body of research on purpose, generativity, relationship, and face-to-face contact makes it plain: engagement with others that flows down the generational chain will make you healthier, happier, and likely longer-lived. It's the real fountain of youth.

Likewise, when we think of what young people need, the answer looks a lot like the assets of the older generation, today and into the future. If we stood in front of a whiteboard and tried to design the perfect human resource for kids, it would be a group that's vast and growing, with time on its hands, inclined toward connection, in possession of abundant skills in areas like emotional regulation, and driven not only to relationship but by generativity. In other words, older people. We don't have to invent that source because it already exists. Mostly we need to stop thwarting its engagement.

Bringing the generations together in ways that involve real, meaningful relationships can chip away at so many problems—from job training to housing, afterschool care to health care, and literacy to loneliness, which some have described as the most significant public health issue of our time. But forging meaningful bonds that connect the generations is not only a means to solving problems; it's an enormously important end.

In her book *The Gardener and the Carpenter,* Alison Gopnik writes that parenting is deeply linked to the human condition, one of a whole set of activities we undertake because they matter in and of themselves. Caregiving for frail elders is another example. Sure, we want to provide this care and support in ways that are cost effective and well managed. But at its root, caregiving is about love and human dignity.

The process of connection across generations is much the same. Experience Corps members connect to kids and help them read better than peers without these bonds, but as I learned, that's just the half of it. In the long run, the love may well be what matters most for both the child and the older person. We know what the older adults get out of it. The younger ones learn to believe in themselves. And once they've had an experience of connection across generations, they're more likely to reproduce that bond for others in their lives.

Every dollar may be spent twice. But every emotion is also felt twice.

That love, that generative heart, is what I witnessed on the pediatrics ward of Maine Medical Center all those many years ago. Aggie and Louise didn't stop desperately ill children from dying. But their presence at those deaths comforted the parents left behind and enriched the human spirit.

I remember so clearly a conversation with Aggie about caring for Susan, a thirteen-year-old girl who knew she would soon die of a congenital heart condition. "She was somebody that you just wanted to reach out to," Aggie said. "Her mom and dad used to come with her, but she'd say, 'I can't talk to them, Aggie, like I can you. I know I am going to die, and I can't talk about that to my mother and father, especially my father.'"

A few weeks later, Aggie said, "Her father called me at about a quarter to three in the morning, and he said, 'Aggie, Susan just died. Can you come?' So I stayed with the family until they removed her body from the hospital, seven or eight hours later. Then I went to Oakfield for the funeral . . . and later the parents sent me her obituary sealed in plastic, and it said, 'Susan is survived by her parents, and by a Foster Grandparent, Aggie Bennett.' That I wouldn't part with for anything."

The boy who wanted to watch his mentor shave, the unprepared college student who racked up nine incompletes, the obituary sealed in plastic. They are all stories about how we, as human beings, care for one another. They are all stories about the alchemy of connection across the generations.

And a reminder that love is truly the legacy we leave behind.

FROM GENERATION TO GENERATION

In my dreams, we get our hands on 10 percent of Singapore's budget for making the most out of the more-old-than-young society. Bill Gates and Oprah come forward not just as wealthy role models doing important and generative things but as spokespeople and catalysts calling their peers to do right by future generations. Presidential candidates pick up JFK's long-dormant challenge and debate ways to move it forward, agreeing on a national Legacy Corps aimed at engaging older people to transform early childhood education in America. And it goes from there!

And then I wake up.

We can't wait for an engraved invitation or the perfectly forged (and endowed) path. Now is the time for us to roll up our sleeves, join with others, and leave our mark. Time is short, and we risk waiting too long.

That conviction led me to launch a new campaign in 2017 to mobilize a million people over fifty to help kids thrive. Enough of the ferment, enough innovation and activity hidden in plain sight. I felt eager—desperate even—to help bring this movement out of the shadows. If our elected officials, renowned celebrities, and billionaires aren't going to do this for us, damn it, we can do it ourselves!

In launching the Generation to Generation (Gen2Gen) campaign, we are working to shine a light on this growing phenomenon, inspire others to join in, and find strength in numbers. We hope to help build a society where older people standing up for younger ones becomes both the expectation and the norm in later life. Our rallying cry: a better future for future generations.

In the first year, tens of thousands came forward. More than 150 organizations have joined in—including big national groups like AARP, Big Brothers Big Sisters, Girls Inc., Year Up, and No Kid Hungry, plus scores of local ones.

Local Gen2Gen organizations have formed, too, bringing advocates for children together to make the best use of older talent in cities including Los Angeles, Boston, Seattle, San Diego, Tampa, and Cincinnati. San Jose mayor Sam Liccardo has taken the lead in his city, creating a local Gen2Gen campaign to "unleash [older adults'] spirit of service, empower their creativity and leverage their professional expertise in support of local youth." San Jose is recruiting a thousand older mentors to help support local youth from low-income families.

And, in the past year alone, some five hundred Encore Fellows have strengthened youth-serving organizations, including Boys and Girls Clubs, Girl Scouts, mentoring groups, and early childhood education institutions.

For me, Gen2Gen is an attempt to bring together the threads of thirty years' work, but of course it's personal, too. I know that I won't likely be doing this work for another thirty years. Looking back, I recognize that I've had the benefit of an extraordinary procession of wise and caring mentors—Gil Stott, Emmy Werner, Aggie and Louise, John Gardner, my own father—and God knows, they've helped me pragmatically, and in spirit too. Gen2Gen is, in part, an expression of gratitude to them and all they've given me and so many others.

Gen2Gen is the chance, too, to come full circle—to focus on helping the most vulnerable young people, the kids whom Experience Corps members reach, whom Emmy Werner studied in Kauai, whom Big Brothers Big Sisters and Foster Grandparents serve. All young people growing up need champions; those growing up against the odds need more of them. I feel the need, the tug of my own generativity, and a responsibility to guide those starting out.

Twenty years ago, Eunice Lin Nichols, then twenty-five, left a job at a consulting firm and followed her heart straight to Experience Corps, where she led our San Francisco team for eleven years. Eager to recreate the intergenerational world so familiar to her while she was growing up as the daughter of Taiwanese immigrants, Eunice has become a leader in the intergenerational cause and the director of the Gen2Gen campaign.

She helped me see that the bond that grew between older and younger at Experience Corps, even between herself and the older Corps members she led, was more than a byproduct of the program; it was its heart. When Eunice talks about her years with Experience Corps, the story extends from the students to the Experience Corps members who threw her first baby shower to the funerals she attended for the members who passed on. The cycle of life again.

I often reflect on how I can try to support Eunice in the way that John Gardner guided me—by listening, offering ideas, trying to provide resources, trusting her to do the work in her own way. I have to say, it's liberating.

I'll even drop my reserve, channel Lucy Kellaway, and say that you should join this multigenerational effort built around purpose and joy, love and legacy. (Even if I won't go as far as Kellaway and tell you to quit your job to do so!) If even a fraction of the one hundred million people over fifty in the United States today do so, imagine the world we could leave behind.

So how can one get started on the quest to live mortal?

Chapter 8

LIVING MORTAL

As the great trumpet player Clark Terry grew older, he became increasingly focused on passing on the jazz tradition to the next generation, serving as the bridge for young musicians to a beautiful past.

Born in 1920, Terry started his career in Count Basie's band before moving on to Duke Ellington's. He mentored Miles Davis and Quincy Jones, along with countless others. Jones considered Terry to be "the top of the list" on trumpet. Dizzy Gillespie judged him to be "one of the greatest, if not, *the* greatest" jazz trumpet player who ever lived. Wynton Marsalis called Terry "the epitome of jazz trumpet, of jazz, and of human kindness."

Terry's pioneering role wasn't restricted to music. He became the first black musician to join NBC's in-house group of musicians in 1960, breaking the late-night color barrier while appearing regularly on *The Tonight Show*.

And he became a great teacher. By 2004, Terry, then eighty-four, was still teaching jazz part-time at William Paterson University and was beginning to lose his eyesight to diabetes. It was in that context that one of his students, Al Hicks, introduced Terry to a blind young piano prodigy and Paterson student from Virginia Beach, Justin Kauflin. Hicks thought Kauflin might be able to help Terry with the struggles that came with encroaching blindness.

"I talked to him just to give him some encouragement," Kauflin told me. "It was a difficult thing for him because he had been afraid of the dark all his life. So for him to go blind was a tough thing to handle." Thus began an extraordinary friendship, chronicled in the documentary film *Keep On Keepin' On,* released in 2014.

Claude Debussy, the classical composer, once said that music is what happens between the notes. That's certainly true with jazz. *Keep On Keepin' On* shows that the idea extends further yet to the mentoring bonds between generations. There are powerful scenes in the film capturing Terry and Kauflin working on the notes. One takes place in the middle of the night, as the younger musician—now in his late twenties—visits Terry at the house he's moved to in rural Arkansas.

Kauflin has made it to the finals of the Thelonious Monk piano competition, a prestigious contest honoring one of Terry's musical collaborators. Filled with doubt and anxiety in anticipation of the competition, Kauflin makes a pilgrimage to see Terry. Age and disease have confined the older musician to a hospital bed at home, with the threat of amputation looming. At Terry's urging, Kauflin sets up a bedside keyboard, and the two rehearse through the night. Kauflin delivers a line; Terry sings alternative ways to play the notes. Time disappears, and a joyous flow comes over the room. At one point, the clock shows 4:00 a.m., as the two go back and forth in a kind of effortless reverie.

For all the focus on the musical notes, there are profound insights to be discerned between them.

"There's so much that I received from Clark that was present in his generation that's not in mine," Kauflin told me, emphasizing the sense of community. "Even just the ability to express your feelings for another person. To hear him say 'I love you' to another musician in a very genuine way and without fear of any sort of negative stigma being attached to it."

Kauflin spoke, too, about what he learned from Clark about investing in relationships.

"I learned, being around him, the value of time," Kauflin said. "With somebody closer to my age, in their thirties or forties. . . . You finish the gig and you go home. But with Clark's generation, the gig was only the beginning. You spent another three or four hours hanging, whether it was at the venue or somewhere else, but to hang was so important to the way of life, and that's where the real friendships were formed and real bonds were made. That's something that's very important to me now, that I want to carry into my performances," Kauflin added. "[I want to] cultivate genuine relationships, not just relationships for the sake of networking . . . spending real quality time with somebody because you just want to and for no other ulterior motive."

As *Keep On Keepin' On* chronicles Terry inching closer and closer to the end, one can feel his urgency to pass on what he's learned to Kauflin burning with a nearly incandescent soulfulness.

As Terry's health continues to deteriorate, he introduces Kauflin to his former student and protégé Quincy Jones, essentially handing him off. Jones goes on to mentor Kauflin and to help advance his career. The film ends at the Montreux Jazz Festival, with Jones presenting the young pianist to the international jazz elite. Kauflin then plays a tribute to Terry, "Song for Clark," to a sustained and rapturous response. It's a moment that reminded me of the applause for Gil Stott that came from dedicating the college commencement address to him all those many years ago.

Terry died in 2015 at the age of ninety-four.

"A lot of people ask, 'Oh, what was the most important lesson Clark gave you? What was the most important thing he said?'" Kauflin told me. "And that always bothers me because the thing that stands out the most is the person he was when I was around him in all the different situations we were in.

"I got to see him on stage and how excellent he was with the audience," Kauflin continued. "I got to see him after the performance and how he interacted with all of the people that wanted to come and say thank you, and how gracious he was no matter what, no matter how tired he was or even how sick he might have felt. It was incredible to witness . . . and then, of course, just to be with him at the house, just relaxing, and still having that joy and that light constantly shining, was something that really sticks with me, more so than anything he ever said."

When *Keep On Keepin' On* was released in 2014, I was in Boston visiting David Shapiro, a friend and the head of MENTOR, a national nonprofit promoting mentoring relationships. He was excited to show me the trailer, which was enough to move me deeply. I wanted to head directly to the theater, but the film had already left Boston. I headed to my next stop, Philadelphia, and missed it there, too. Finally, the following week, I traveled to the Chicago Ideas Festival to be part of a session on longevity and its implications. On the other side of town, at the Music Box Theatre (appropriately), *Keep On Keepin' On* was in the midst of a brief run.

So run I did. Out of the session into the late afternoon winter light, into a cab, racing to catch a 4:00 p.m. show. I found my seat just as the house lights were dimming. When the film ended, there was complete silence for half a minute; then the audience stood up and clapped. Afterward Justin Kauflin appeared with his black Lab, Candy, by his side, to talk about Clark Terry and to answer audience questions. I got to meet him the following year when he performed at an Encore.org event at the San Francisco Jazz Center. And we spoke later about the influence Terry had on his life.

To this day, the film has a deep emotional hold on me. It conveys much of what I've been trying to communicate throughout this book and captures so many important lessons about how to nurture the next generation.

So what is it that we can learn from the Clark Terrys of the world, these masters of what matters? What can we discern about how to be generative and how to live on, even if we aren't charismatic superheroes born with a gift for this role?

If you're hoping for advice, I want to let you down easy. Truthfully, I've never much trusted self-help books or advice, particularly my own. When people ask me questions about their next steps in life, I'm often at a loss. I've got no formula, blueprint, or ten-point plan.

That said, I have collected thoughts from spending time talking with, observing, and simply being in the presence of an extraordinary group of individuals over several decades who are making a monument out of what were once the leftover years. I've seen, too, that flowing downhill can be a lifestyle—a collection of small choices and big decisions about how and where to live.

So here are some of the observations that have left an impression on me, that I come back to again and again in my own life. *Caveat emptor.*

Accept mortality.

John F. Kennedy never saw his fiftieth birthday, but he had a lot of wise things to say about the value of longevity, how to live fully in the second half of life, and what it means to be human. "Our most basic common link is that we all inhabit this planet," he said. "We all breathe the same air. We all cherish our children's future. And we are all mortal."

Living mortal starts with *being mortal,* with accepting that life is a journey with a beginning, a middle, and an end—and that is as it should be. The wealthy "immortalists" in Silicon Valley who are trying to put an end to *the* end are just wasting time, time they're going to wish they had back someday.

Yes, the death rate holds steady at 100 percent—and we need to lean into life's great teacher, not because we should embrace morose darkness, but because when all "falls away," we know what our priorities are, what matters, and what endures.

In the past, wisdom may have been wasted on the old. Just when we came to acquire a deeper perspective on life, we were too sick and worn out—and rejected by society—to do much with it. That's no longer true, and that's the essence of the living mortal opportunity we have today—that sweet spot in the life course when we know what matters and have the time to do something with that knowledge.

We can make our bucket list and check a few things off. We can consider carefully where and how we want to live, with whom, doing what. We can decide to steer our lives toward what David Brooks calls the "eulogy virtues"—by knowing exactly how we'd like to be remembered and behaving accordingly. (I've long thought somebody should develop a eulogy app. It could prompt us to think about how we'd like to be remembered, then provide a GPS-like function that periodically tells us whether we're on or off course.)

Ultimately, we have the chance to see past the illusion of endless time, plant some new seeds, give away what we've learned, and foment hope in the next generation before we depart for a different land.

Let's not waste it.

Prepare for a new life stage.

Nobody wants to gain weight, go bald, get wrinkles, deal with a two-minute delay (make that three) when it comes to remembering names, or turn the TV up to its loudest setting. Certainly no one wants to become frail and infirm. But the most satisfied people I know are the ones who welcome this new, encore stage of life beyond the middle years, prepare for it, and lean into its unique features to find happiness.

Carl Jung once wrote: "Wholly unprepared, [people] embark upon the second half of life . . . with the false presupposition that our truths and ideas will serve us as hitherto. But we cannot live the afternoon of life according to the programme of life's morning—for what was great in the morning will be little at evening, and what in the morning was true will at evening have become a lie."

Today, the seduction of living life's afternoon according to the morning's program continues to be ever present. Resist! Rather than running so hard from the generative purpose of our current life stage, we need to embrace it. Jung himself warned about the perils of becoming "eternal adolescents." We need to take this stage on its own terms, as a time with its own integrity.

This can be a daunting effort on our own. All these years after Jung called for them, there are still too few vehicles to help prepare us to live the second half of life to its fullest. Where is the gap year for grown-ups, one designed to help us catch our breath, wrestle with the priorities for the coming period, and make generativity a central priority for the next phase of life? We need time to square up to this period and to the role we want to play with younger generations.

There are emerging models of how we might choose to include generativity in our lives. Chip Conley, who created the Joie de Vivre hotel chain and ultimately sold it in his fifties before becoming the head of strategy at Airbnb, describes the role of a "modern elder." In his new job at the travel start-up, he became a real-life version of the Robert De Niro character in *The Intern*—one half wise sage, the other half beginner's mind. He found that he could offer the wisdom of his experience as a mentor to his younger colleagues while also learning a fresh mind-set for strategy and business. Conley is now at work on a retreat center, the Modern Elder Academy, designed to help people in midlife rethink their lives and careers.

For the past couple of years, I've worked with various clergy who are trying to develop spiritually rooted opportunities for this kind of post-midlife course correction and to ensure this period is devoted to living a legacy.

Ruth Wooden, who led the Ad Council before returning to school in her sixties to get a master's in spiritual counseling, has created the Encore Transition Program at Union Theological Seminary. A version of this effort is now under way at another theological seminary in the Twin Cities. Laura Geller, an emeritus rabbi in Los Angeles—and the third woman to be confirmed as a Reform rabbi in the United States—is laying the groundwork for a bar and bat mitzvah–like rite for sixty-somethings focused on leaving the world better than we found it.

For many, this new stage of life will last for thirty years or more. It's worth taking the time to think about what matters most to us in this period—and prepare for a new course. That may mean going back to school, becoming an intern or fellow, or launching a do-it-yourself journey. The cost can be a stumbling block, but a year of renewal focused on how to live a legacy may be worth it when compared to underwriting decades of retirement.

Focus on relationships.
I know that I've been rather ardent about this point, but I think it bears repeating.

All too often, our efforts to develop the next generation take the form of honing the skills and competencies of young people. That's obviously important, but I don't think it's the only—or even the most valuable—contribution we can make. The central lesson I learned from my work on mentoring is that we often get our priorities reversed. At Experience Corps, we were so focused on reading scores—not unimportant—that we sometimes assumed building the bonds between Experience Corps members and kids was secondary. I now believe that honing literacy skills was actually the vehicle around which an equally important objective was built: the relationship. In other words, the means also turned out to be the end.

This is not to say that help with reading, meals, or instrumental connections should be ignored. Clark Terry introduces Justin Kauflin to an earlier protégé, Quincy Jones, as Terry is nearing the end of his life, keen to help the young man build his career. John Gardner connected me to the investors who would underwrite the bulk of our work for a decade and a half. I don't in any way want to diminish these important dimensions.

That said, I'll never forget the time, after John Gardner had passed, that one of his assistants and close advisers told me that John considered me the "son he never had." (Gardner had two wonderful daughters.) I'm not sure I've been more moved by anything in my life.

In the words of George Vaillant, "Relationships matter most. Full stop."

Get proximate.

Along with recognizing our mortality, realizing the unique impera-tives of the encore phase, and preparing developmentally to be more generative, we can take steps to reject age segregation.

I don't mean marching outside Sun City and urging residents to repent. I suggest thinking long and hard about the way we set up our lives. For dec-ades now, older people have been encouraged, incentivized, and pressured to spend their lives apart from younger generations—through age-segregated housing, geographic moves to communities overwhelmingly composed of older people, senior centers, peer-focused activities, and even some volun-teer programs that serve in the end to cut us off from young people.

If we want to stay connected to younger generations, including family and those beyond our immediate kin, we need to be conscious about housing, activities, religious congregations, and the other places where we spend our time. Just being physically proximate mat-ters. My friend Courtney Martin moved to a cohousing complex in Oakland, where she got to know her eighty-year-old neighbor, Louise Dunlap, who has become one of the pillars of her life. If Louise had opted instead for a senior housing community, this opportunity would never have been possible.

Same with Suzanne Schecker, a therapist who conducts her practice out of her cottage at Treehouse, the village in western Massachusetts dedicated to supporting families who are raising foster kids. "Being in an intergenerational community is an amazing experience," she told me, "because you get to live with the entire human development spec-trum. You get to see all of it. You get to be with children again, and it reminds you of your own childhood. And you get to experience your neighbors and what they're going through. We've buried people and we've seen babies come into the world here."

But it's not just where we live that's important. Clark Terry decided to focus on jazz education in his seventies and set up shop at a uni-versity, which ensured he would be in the regular presence of young people. Others, like Experience Corps members, volunteer regularly in elementary schools and libraries. Some, like former president Jimmy Carter, teach in religious schools. My older neighbors, Jake and Joyce, find ways to spend time with the neighborhood kids.

When you spend time with your children and grandchildren, you're interacting with the next generations. When you reach beyond family to teach knitting, coach soccer, or joke with kids from your front steps or porch, you're there for children who can always use another caring adult in their corner. And they're there for you, too, keeping you connected to whatever's coming next, satisfying that need you have to be needed and to nurture a legacy.

Listen up.

I remember buying a book of StoryCorps stories a number of years ago with the title *Listening Is an Act of Love*. How true. That was one of the first lessons we learned from the Big Brothers Big Sisters research all those many years ago. Young people want mentors who show up—and who, for the most part, shut up. They want mentors who are focused on listening much more than talking.

Research on what young people are looking for in relationships with adults bears this out. At the top of the list is listening, followed by providing useful, concrete help. At the bottom: imparting advice. America's Promise Alliance researchers at Boston University found that emotional support (love and caring) and instrumental support (like providing a ride or babysitting) are the factors most likely to increase the number of young people who graduate from high school.

The 2016 study—"Don't Quit on Me: What Young People Who Left School Say About the Power of Relationships"—puts listening first among its recommendations for those who want to help. "Young people are looking for stable connections they can depend on, not just to care about them, but also to do something for them so they can do more for themselves. They also say they're looking for support from people who respect what they're facing and offer a helping hand without judgment."

John Gardner used to talk about how easy and seductive it is to be interesting. The much harder but more worthwhile trait is *being interested*. He admitted that he spent the first half of his life cultivating the former. It was only as he matured that Gardner realized that to become an effective mentor and leader he needed to become much better at the latter. I remember Harold "Doc" Howe, the commissioner of education under Gardner at the US Department of Health, Education, and Welfare, recalling that when he'd go in to see John, Gardner would ask him to sit, and then simply say, "What's on your mind?" And Howe would have his undivided attention.

It's hard not to be struck by the quantity of listening in *Keep On Keepin' On*. It's there because of the depth of the relationship but also because both Kauflin and Terry are blind musicians, dependent on listening for so much of their personal and professional lives.

The value of listening fits well with another trait—patience. The Big Brothers Big Sisters research found that the mentors who swooped in with an efficient plan for turning a young person's life around were dismal failures. The children were hiding from them; only 9 percent of these pairs were meeting at the end of a year. But with age we get wiser and less hurried with things we value. I remember interviewing Experience Corps members who had all the time in the world for the students—and little time for researchers like me. They valued their time in a way that led to focusing on what mattered most.

Many of us also have more time in this stage of our lives to spend building and maintaining relationships. At the time I got to know him, John Gardner was less in demand, less rushed. I'm not sure that he would have had time for me earlier in his life. Justin Kauflin said much the same thing about his relationship with Clark Terry. Although he first met Terry as a college student, when the great trumpeter was still teaching multiple students and working on other projects in New York, the two didn't develop a deep friendship and mentoring bond until Justin started visiting Terry in Arkansas, where he'd moved to simplify his life, lower costs, and focus on his health.

Find creative ways to connect.

So often, technology is blamed for driving people, particularly young and old, apart. But there are ways to use technology to connect across distance and generations—and actually feed face-to-face connection.

My favorite recent example is the story of twenty-two-year-old African American rapper Spencer Sleyon, from East Harlem, and his unlikely bond with Rosalind Guttman, an eighty-one-year-old white, Jewish retiree living in Florida. The two met entirely by accident, when Words with Friends, the Scrabble-like app, randomly assigned them to play each other. They played hundreds of games, battling for points (kids versus canes?) and getting to know one another in the process. A bond developed. When they finally parted, the older woman left Spencer with these words: "Whatever you want out of life, just go grab it."

Later, Amy Butler, the senior minister of Riverside Church in New York, whose son is a friend of Sleyon's, overheard the young man say, "My best friend is an eighty-one-year-old white woman who lives in a retirement community in Florida." Butler determined to bring the two together, and the resulting trip to Palm Beach produced genuine closeness and ease, plus a wave of media attention. Guttman called it "one of the most memorable days of my life."

Words with Friends aside, there are a number of more deliberate ways to connect with young people virtually. Strive for College, for example, helps people of all ages become online mentors to high school students who are applying for college and need help with their applications.

"I love learning about young people's lives," says longtime journalist and Strive for College mentor Karen Sughrue, "and convincing them that they have a great story to tell. I mentored one student, who had excelled in her high school ROTC training program. That alone makes a good start to a story. But in probing her family background,

I learned she was the daughter of a single mom who had emigrated from Haiti with great ambitions for her children, and had a brother serving in the US military. We were able to work all that into her essay about how college will help her become the leader she wants to be in the future."

The virtual opportunity offered by Strive for College gives Sughrue a chance to use her experience to help kids on her own time, and she's enjoying it. "It's fun to see the world from a teenager's perspective again, and it's so rewarding when a student writes back and says, 'You've helped me SO much!'"

Live on by letting go.

Clark Terry imparted a deep influence on Justin Kauflin's approach to jazz over years of working together. But Terry's goal was not to shape Kauflin into a musician who sounds like him. It was to provide Kauflin with the confidence and counsel to sound like *himself*.

We've all had bosses who micromanage, causing us to doubt our own abilities, fear risk and failure, and avoid making even the smallest decisions. Being truly generative means doing the opposite, using our experience and accumulated wisdom, such as it is, to instill confidence in others, help them embrace risk and failure as the best route to learning, and do whatever it takes to find their own path to their own destination.

Randy Pausch, the late computer science professor at Carnegie Mellon who delivered *The Last Lecture* after getting a diagnosis of terminal cancer, was very clear on this point. "So my dreams for my kids are very exact: I want them to find their own path to fulfillment. And given that I won't be there, I want to make this clear: Kids, don't try to figure out what I wanted you to become. I want you to become what *you* want to become."

John Gardner certainly showed me the way. He passed on the Experience Corps name, core idea, and mantle but didn't dictate how the program would be shaped. He instead showed his faith in me,

Linda Fried, Tom Endres, and our team, and set about getting us the resources and connections that would contribute to success.

Find the change maker within.
So many of the preceding ideas are built around setting ourselves up to be in multigenerational settings and to connect with younger people in ways that support them; enhance the likelihood of forming deeper, enduring connections; and contribute to a virtuous cycle of life. But for all the importance of connection, there is also a need for innovation—and not just at the grand level of a country like Singapore or a venture like Now Teach.

As I've traveled the country over the past decades, and particularly over the past year, I've encountered so many individuals who are doing creative things—large and small—that build bridges across the generations, contribute to a better world, and inspire others to do the same.

Take Hal Garman, a retired minister in his eighties, who moved into a community for seniors in a suburb of Washington, DC, but then, instead of retreating behind the gates, took an interest in "the kids living just outside our fence." He recruited more than one hundred fellow residents to serve as afterschool mentors to local third, fourth, and fifth graders. In return, every week throughout the school year, the children visit the elders for dinner and joint activities.

Or Rey Castuciano, the young son of Filipino immigrants, who started Table Wisdom to pair English-speaking older adults, often suffering from loneliness, with college students who don't speak English as a first language, for conversations in person or via videoconference. The older adults remain socially active; the students get older mentors while improving their English and expanding their networks.

I have long been struck by the power of older people who combine experience and creativity to make huge changes in the lives of others, frequently children. For ten years, Encore.org ran the Purpose Prize (now run by AARP) to honor and invest in older social innovators, half of whom focused their efforts on young people. Winners have helped young people behind bars get ready for life and work after incarceration, used the arts to help teens deal with the trauma of gun violence, even created giving circles among affluent elders who donate their Social Security checks to support early childhood education. Oftentimes, these older innovators launched their start-ups as part of intergenerational teams, changing the world while passing the torch.

As impressive as these trailblazers are, my point is that the rest of us don't have to single-handedly change the world to be change makers. We can all initiate efforts and actions in our lives, large and small, with and for young people, that influence small groups of people or even one person at a time.

It all matters. As Michelle Kuo writes about her experiences as a young teacher in the Mississippi delta, "The rational thought, would be to say to myself, *You can't do that much, you're not that important, there are so many forces in a person's life, good and bad, who do you think you are?* That's what I said to make myself feel better after I left the Delta, and sometimes I still say it. But then what is a human for? A person must matter to another, it must mean something for two people to have passed time together, to have put work into each other and into becoming more fully themselves."

Combine purpose and a paycheck.
The finances of longer lives are daunting to most people, myself included. There are the scary truths about how little most boomers have saved, how many people enter retirement earlier than they planned, and how few are prepared for a new chapter that could last for thirty or forty years. I hear equal trepidation about a lack of purpose in the second half of life. After a full career and maybe even a gap year for grown-ups, what's next?

Many people need and want some combination of paid work and new purpose as they head into the period opening up beyond the middle years. For over a decade we've been using the term "encore career" to describe second acts for the greater good—jobs that combine purpose, passion, and a paycheck.

Our research shows that some 4.5 million individuals over fifty have navigated their way into these encore careers, many focused on developing the next generation. Another 21 million give doing so high priority. Research shows that these second acts last about a decade. Put these numbers together, and they add up to about 250 million years of potential contribution to creating a better world. Hardly a glancing contribution.

Baltazar Villalba found his encore in the classroom. Arriving in the United States at age five, he struggled in school as a first-generation English learner. But he persevered, ultimately attending California Polytechnic University. He graduated in eight years, while working full-time at night, living out an attenuated version of the American dream.

Villalba began his career as an aerospace engineer, then transferred into marketing, where he worked for decades at tech giants Hewlett Packard and IBM. Along the way, he had an urge to guide young students like his former self. In what he describes as a "now or never" moment, Villalba started searching for a way to follow his impulse.

He discovered the EnCorps STEM Teachers Program, which helps midlife professionals earn teaching credentials with a combination of course work and early teaching experience, while filling a critical need for math and science teachers. EnCorps was launched by Sherry Lansing, who started her career as a math teacher, then became the first woman to lead a Hollywood movie studio.

Villalba applied, was accepted, and began teaching middle school math in Watts, California. After a year, he found a job at Soledad Enrichment Action, which turned out to be exactly what he was looking for.

"It's so much more satisfying than what I used to do for work," he said. "I feel comfortable with the students. Some of them may look intimidating, but they're just kids. They just want someone to listen to them and believe in them. I get to be the male figure in their lives who says, 'You can be an engineer.'"

COMING HOME

Kareem Abdul-Jabbar, arguably the greatest basketball player of the twentieth century, is a lifetime jazz aficionado. When his Los Angeles house tragically burned to the ground in 1983, the fire took with it Abdul-Jabbar's three thousand jazz albums, one of the most significant collections of its type in the world, with undoubtedly many of Clark Terry's records.

The basketball player's love of jazz was inherited. Born Ferdinand Lewis Alcindor Jr., he was the son of New York police lieutenant Ferdinand Lewis Alcindor Sr., a one-time Juilliard student and an accomplished jazz trombonist who played with some of the same bands as Terry, including Count Basie's.

Abdul-Jabbar, the most sought-after high school basketball player in 1965, was long inclined to attend UCLA, in part because that's where Jackie Robinson had starred as a college athlete. But his decision was sealed when he met John Wooden, the school's varsity basketball coach. Wooden's message to him had nothing to do with sports, athletic stardom, fancy cars, or any other perks. "You're a good student," Wooden told him, "and I think you'll thrive academically at UCLA." It stood out.

In his 2017 book, *Coach Wooden and Me: Our 50-Year Friendship On and Off the Court,* Abdul-Jabbar explains that Wooden always thought of himself as a teacher, not a coach—and that is how their relationship was first forged. Wooden was unrivaled at basketball strategy but equally gifted at leadership and motivation. He drove his teams exceptionally hard, but Abdul-Jabbar describes him as being masterful at criticizing without creating resentment.

Abdul-Jabbar describes one of the great coach-player relationships in the history of sports. Together Wooden and Abdul-Jabbar won three straight NCAA titles, winning eighty-eight games while losing only two during three years together. Their story is likewise one of the most profound—and mutual—mentoring relationships of our time.

By all accounts, they were an odd couple. Photos depicting the two together in the 1960s show a seven-foot-one Abdul-Jabbar (then Alcindor), a young African American from New York, soon to convert to Orthodox Islam, boycott the 1968 Olympics on racial grounds, become the all-time leading scorer in the NBA, and write twelve books, most on social justice and African American history.

Next to him is the five-foot-ten Wooden, barely reaching Abdul-Jabbar's chest, a star college basketball player at one time himself—in fact, the first player to be an All-American three years in a row. Clean cut, impeccably attired, and Midwestern to the core, Wooden required his players to adhere to a strict dress code and was unfailingly polite and old school in appearance and manner. He would become the winner of ten NCAA championships in twelve years, including seven in a row, the most successful basketball coach in history.

Like Terry and Kauflin's bond, the relationship between Abdul-Jabbar and Wooden took time to unfold and develop. At first it was defined by Wooden as a skilled teacher and motivator. Then by Abdul-Jabbar, as his experiences as a black man taught Wooden about the pain of racism.

Over time their connection ripened into a close friendship. Once Abdul-Jabbar was traded from the Milwaukee Bucks to the Los Angeles Lakers, the two would hang out together in Wooden's den. They watched western movies, argued over baseball, and talked about books. Both loved literature.

Finally, during a period of great heartbreak, when Abdul-Jabbar lost his mother and Wooden lost his wife of fifty-three years, they became each other's primary source of support. Looking back, the younger man has written: "I could feel the difference whenever I went to sit with him in his den. . . . Before, it had felt like I was visiting a friend." According to Abdul-Jabbar, "Now it felt like I was coming home."

Wooden died in 2010 at the age of ninety-nine. But Abdul-Jabbar writes that he still feels that his late friend, mentor, and coach is teaching him. His words and perspective come back even as the now-seventy-one-year-old Abdul-Jabbar makes important decisions and faces challenges, including leukemia.

"This book is not just an appreciation of our friendship or an acknowledgment of Coach Wooden's deep influence on my life," Abdul-Jabbar has said. "It is the realization that some lives are so extraordinary and touch so many people that their story must be told to generations to come so that those values aren't diminished or lost altogether."

The mutuality of the Abdul-Jabbar–Wooden relationship recalls the Terry-Kauflin bond. Kauflin fails at the Thelonious Monk competition, but Terry serves as his backstop. There is a poignant scene in *Keep On Keepin' On* where Kauflin expresses his heartfelt appreciation for all the time, help, and support Terry has lavished on him. At Terry's side in the hospital, as the old man lies in bed, Kauflin simply says, "Thank you so much, CT." To which Terry responds, "Thank you . . . thank God for you."

Years later, when Wendy Oxenhorn of the Jazz Foundation of America introduced Kauflin at a performance, she described him as "the man who helped keep Clark alive the last few years, who gave him a reason to live."

Epilogue
WE WAIT TOO LONG

At the Hyowon Healing Center in Seoul, South Korea, men and women come to experience their own mortality. At these regular and somber events financed by a funeral company, first the center shows an inspirational video; then a staff member delivers a lecture about death. Participants are each photographed in traditional clothing for the pictures that will go on their coffins. Then, wearing the garments in which they will be laid to rest, they are ushered into a candlelit room lined with caskets.

Each coffin has a desk beside it, complete with a tissue box for the inevitable emotions. Participants write out final reflections that will be read at a mock funeral to be conducted for each of them, with the rest serving as mourners.

Next, the lights are dimmed, and everyone lies down in a coffin, soon nailed shut by a priestly attendant, "the Envoy from the Other World." For ten (often very long) minutes, the coffins remain shut. Participants are told to reflect on their lives, on memories, on what matters, on what they wish they had accomplished. It is completely dark, with little air; the experience closely mimics the circumstances that precede cremation.

Finally, the caskets are opened to light and air—and life. According to the *New York Times,* the leader of the ceremony states, "Now, you have shed your old self. You are reborn to have a fresh start!" Since 2012, more than fifteen thousand people have had mock funerals here, written out their thoughts, and gone through this free death experience.

I thought about traveling to Seoul and going to the Hyowon Healing Center to experience my own funeral. What a way to bring the eulogy virtues into focus. At Encore.org, we work with the mayor of Seoul, who is determined to turn his jurisdiction into a shining city on a hill, showcasing the best use of older adults' talents to solve social problems and groom the next generation. I suspect his office could have gotten me into my own temporary coffin.

But before I could plan the trip, reality intervened.

My beloved father died. He was eighty-six years old, suffering from decades of wear and tear resulting from diabetes, his decline paralleling Clark Terry's own suffering from the same disease. A few months earlier, my father had faced a terrible choice: lose his leg from an uncontrolled infection or skip the operation and go into hospice care. He was clearly close to the end, in a horrible cycle of infection-induced emergency room visits, followed by weeks in the hospital, months in a rehab facility, and a brief bout at home before the rotation repeated itself yet again.

All the while my father had become completely deaf, his hearing loss mounting over the previous decade, in the process cutting him off more and more from others. And it was clear, too, that he was succumbing steadily to dementia. In his final year, he slept most of the time, his rest punctuated by brief, hazy periods out of the stupor. Visits would often consist of watching him doze, interrupted from time to time by a surprise episode of consciousness.

One Sunday morning, after a few days visiting him in Philadelphia, I had an hour left before heading to the airport to fly home. I read by his bedside while he slept. Suddenly, he was awake and, as always, smiling broadly. (The nurses at the hospitals and nursing homes universally loved him for his warmth and upbeat demeanor.)

"Marc!" he exclaimed, breaking into a vast grin. I suspect he was so happy to see his own son, instead of the usually empty, antiseptic, fluorescent-lit room. "You're so good to me!" he proclaimed in a joyous and heartfelt tone.

I reflexively responded, "*You're* so good to me!" And I meant it, because he was a real give-you-the-shirt-off-his-back guy. He nodded—then dove right back into a coma-like state.

The idea of putting him through an amputation, traumatic for even the healthiest person, seemed cruel. To me, he was barely alive. In fact, during those final months, when I was asked how he was doing, I used to say that he was already 90 percent deceased, slowly fading away for years.

We opted for hospice care. Yet there was the nagging question about what my father himself would have wanted. Throughout his life, he was not particularly good at facing up to harsh realities. I'm not sure if he ever accepted his coming death. I wouldn't be surprised if he believed that somehow he would recover, as impossible as that prospect might have been.

When the hospice nurses told my sister, who was by his side at the end, that it was a matter of days, maybe even hours, I decided to come ahead of the rest of my family, with only my youngest son, Micah, seven at the time. My father had hung on for so long that I didn't scramble to catch the very next flight but assumed that we might be there for days before he passed.

But on the five-hour flight east, I checked my email obsessively, more and more anxious that the end was coming. Just before we landed, there was a message from my sister, Lisa, that he had died.

My sister had told him that I was coming with his grandson and would be there in a few hours. My father seemed to rally, she said. His breathing picked up briefly. One of his eyes opened halfway. But he couldn't hang on.

Was he able to hear my sister and understand what she was saying? Or were these reactions simply reflexive responses to the impending shutdown of his system? I don't know. But I know that I should have been by his side in those final moments.

The next time I saw my father, he was laid out in a casket. His waxy body was freezing to the touch, his facial features stretched into a pained expression. He didn't look like himself.

But as we headed to the memorial service, I was struck by how much the final reflections were in his spirit.

My father had not felt very successful in life. Right out of college, he'd followed his dream of becoming a gym teacher. He was a naturally generous and generative person, good with his students, beloved by his children and his grandchildren, who to my surprise celebrated what would have been his eighty-seventh birthday a few months ago with a cake and happy memories of the man.

Yet throughout his life, he was plagued by a social context that didn't much value his impulse to be an educator, to develop the next generation, to invest in kids. I remember Woody Allen's line from *Annie Hall*: "Those who can't do teach, and those who can't teach, teach gym."

Soon, for need of money, my father traded in his classroom for an administrator's desk. Then, at age sixty, he was compelled to take the offer he couldn't refuse—85 percent of his salary for life if he accepted early retirement, a Philadelphia school district incentive to shed higher-salaried employees. So just as Experience Corps was taking flight in Philadelphia, my father was being shown the exit, for essentially being too old.

Oddly, that exit turned out to be a source of liberation. A star sprinter and high jumper as a student, he had a lifetime love of track and field. For forty years straight he was an official at the Penn Relays, one of the nation's most prestigious track-and-field competitions. He mostly served as a pole vault official, but in 1976 when American Dwight Stones broke the world high-jump record at the Penn Relays and ended up on the cover of *Sports Illustrated,* my father was in the background staring up at Stones's soaring figure.

In honor of my father's durability, the *Philadelphia Daily News* published a feature article about him, during his twenty-second consecutive year officiating at the Penn Relays. Its title: "You Can Bank on His Presence at the Vaults." In the piece, he explained that one of the joys of the Penn Relays for him was watching fourth and fifth graders compete alongside master athletes in their seventies and eighties.

After taking his early retirement package, my father started substitute teaching while also organizing track meets for elementary school students—in both cases, a return to his roots. He continued doing this work into his eighties, teaching gym to urban high school students, organizing events for the little kids, and loving both.

For all the more vaunted mentors I've had over the years, I realize that my life's work has really been inspired by his life's work and, most especially, the way he handled what could have been golden years characterized by play or leftover years marked by boredom.

My father's last decades were a time of great fulfillment for him, even if they were hardly the norm. After all, he could have been living in a condo on a golf course in Florida or Arizona, surrounded by fellow seniors, whiling away the hours playing games rather than staying home in Philadelphia helping young people do so.

Although my father's ethos may not have been widely practiced in recent decades, it became clear to me at his memorial service that he was living out an enduring truth, reflected in long-standing traditions. The clergyman didn't know my father; still, he went through the expected homages to what a good, kind person he was—and he was. But it was in the readings and prayers that I felt my father's spirit most fully emerge.

One passage, entitled "The Acorn," comes from the Talmud. It tells the story of a rabbi passing through a field, noticing an old man planting an acorn.

"Why are you planting that acorn?" the rabbi asks, in what I imagine is a scoffing tone. "You surely do not expect to live long enough to see it grow into an oak tree."

To which the old man—turning slowly from the ground to fix his glance on the not-so-wise clergyman—says, "My ancestors planted seeds so that I might enjoy the shade and the fruit of trees. I do likewise for those who come after me."

It sounded so familiar to me. For years, I'd been quoting a Greek proverb that reads, "Society grows great when older people plant trees under whose shade they shall never sit."

I see now that this book has been all about planting seeds, irrigating them, letting life bloom, and cultivating gardens, from the Treehouse Project onward. It's ironic that my own great mentor in much of this was a man named Gardner.

Planting, tending, bequeathing to the next generation—it's the essential human project, one we've long understood yet let slip over the past half century. It is our role as older people to plant those trees under whose shade we shall never sit. Our task is not to try to be young, but to be there for those who actually are.

Given the new demographics and longevity, embracing this role is the only way we can survive as a society. And it is, as it has always been, the root of happiness and fulfillment in the later stages of life. For the real fountain of youth is the fountain with youth. And the only true way to live forever is to live together, not only in the present but from generation to generation. Now more than ever.

My father's memorial concluded with a second reading, "We Wait Too Long," which, as you might imagine given my lifelong struggle with deadlines, also touched me deeply.

"Death has claimed a loved one," it opens, "thus reminding us of our own mortality." It continues with a litany of examples all serving to underscore that our own time on earth is finite and that we have a responsibility to the future.

We wait too long to show kindness,
To speak words of gratitude and concern. . . .
We wait too long to set aside selfishness,
To give of our time and to share our bounty. . . .
We wait too long to give the love
Which may no longer be needed tomorrow.

And then the prayer calls us to action.

> *In tribute to our departed, let us now resolve,*
> *To wait no longer, to delay no more;*
> *Rather, let us begin to do now,*
> *Those good things which can be done today.*

Let that be our resolution, out of gratitude for all that was planted before us, to do right by future generations, leave the world better than we found it, and begin to do so this day.

AUTHOR'S NOTE

There are tens of millions of adults over fifty who stand up and show up for young people every day—childcare providers, teachers, medical workers, nonprofit staff and volunteers, elected leaders, faith leaders, business leaders, and more. And yet the prevailing story about older adults in our country today is often one of selfishness, entitlement(s), and need. If you believe there's a different story to tell—one of purpose, love, and engagement across the generations—please join Encore.org's Generation to Generation campaign at iamgen2gen. org or write to us at hello@iamgen2gen.org. Together we can help realize the potential of longer lives and the potential of every child. Together we can tell a new story.

ACKNOWLEDGMENTS

This book is animated from start to finish by deep gratitude for a set of wise and caring mentors: Gil Stott, John Gardner, Emmy Werner, Aggie Bennett and Louise Casey, Phyllis Moen, Ellen Goodman, Peter Osnos, Mike Bailin, and Ed Speedling. They've made an enormous difference in my life and the lives of countless others.

I've been inspired deeply, as well, by my father, Bernard Freedman, who passed away while I was writing this book. He was a wonderful man, a bastion of kindness throughout his life, thoroughly dedicated to his own children and grandchildren and to the children of others.

No one had a bigger or more valuable impact on the writing and thinking in this book than my colleague at Encore.org, Stefanie Weiss, editor extraordinaire and chief thought partner throughout. Her wordcraft was matched by extraordinary patience—and an ability to keep my spirits afloat when I was losing battles with the blank screen.

I was likewise buoyed and enlightened throughout by a group of close friends and advisers who guided the project: John Gomperts, Ellen Goodman (again), Marci Alboher, Carol Larson, David Bornstein, Joe Plummer, Phyllis Segal, Eunice Nichols, Paul Irving, Paul Taylor, Lester Strong, Andrew Scott, Joe McCannon, Bill Damon, Anne Colby, Judy Mohraz, Trent Stamp, and Laura Carstensen. And to Eric Liu for his overall wisdom and inspiration and for suggesting the book's title.

If only I'd been able to follow the other half of their wise counsel, this would have been a much better book. I am immensely grateful for all their generosity of time and ideas.

I want to express my gratitude to another group I owe a great debt of thanks: the people who know so much about creating interdependence among the generations and took the time to tell their stories to me. This group includes Nancy Henkin (a mentor as well), Donna Butts, Justin Kauflin, Susan Lavigne, Grant Woods, Heidi Speed, Leng Leng Thang, Peter and Cathy Whitehouse, Cherry Hendrix, Judy Cockerton, Annie Benedetti, Steve Minter, Laura Berick, Ward Greene, Steve Higgs, Noelle Marcus, Rachel Goor, Catalina Garcia, Chris Forsyth, Sherlyn Lee, Sister Geraldine Tan, Katherine Wilcox, Doug Collins, and Gina Logan.

I benefited from two fellowships, the first at the Stanford Center on Longevity and the second at the David and Lucile Packard Foundation; both provided supportive, thoughtful colleagues and room to develop this book. Joy Zhang and Madeline Dangerfield-Cha of the Stanford Graduate School of Business provided invaluable research assistance. I'm likewise grateful to Glenn Ruffenach, Cristina Lourosa, and Demetria Gallegos at the *Wall Street Journal* and Sarah Green Carmichael at *Harvard Business Review,* who provided opportunities to work through and publish ideas that would eventually find their way into this manuscript, as well as to TEDxSanFrancisco for providing the vehicle to piece together these elements.

Support for this work was provided by a generous group of funders who underwrote this project and related work, including the Packard Foundation (Carol Larson, Jeff Sunshine, Carlin Johnson-Politzer, Meera Mani, Chris DeCardy, Cathy Winter, and Karla Scheire); the Einhorn Family Charitable Trust (Jennifer Hoos-Rothberg and Jon Gruber); the John Templeton Foundation (Kimon Sargeant); the Eisner Foundation (Trent Stamp and Cathy Choi); the Schultz Family Foundation (Daniel Pitasky and Michael Brotchner); the Smith Charitable Trust (Laura Mason); the Deerbrook Charitable Trust (Art Sundstrom and Larry Clark); the MetLife Foundation (Dennis White); and Rik Kranenburg and Diane Paul. Although not involved directly in this project, the Atlantic Philanthropies underwrote much of the earlier work that flowed into it. I owe enormous gratitude to Atlantic's remarkable founder, Chuck Feeney, and the foundation's supportive staff.

Another deep debt is to friends and colleagues at AARP, most of all Jo Ann Jenkins—the CEO and author of the book *Disrupt Aging*, which had a big impact on my thinking—as well as Kevin Donnellan and Barb Quaintance. I also want to thank my colleagues in the creation of Experience Corps, Linda Fried and Tom Endres.

I'd like to acknowledge a set of intellectual influences, including Alison Gopnik, Atul Gawande, Dan McAdams, and Howard Chudacoff, none of whom I've met but all of whom have had a big impact on my own outlook. Thanks also to Cathy Ventura-Merkle, David Bank, Lew Feldstein, Ken Dychtwald, Nancy Morrow-Howell, Chip Conley, Robert Putnam, Sally Osberg, David Shapiro, Andrew Blechman, Bill Thomas, Alex Harris, Rob Gurwitt, Joe Coughlin, Jonathan Rauch, Jane Isaacs Lowe, Rick Moody, Andy Achenbaum, Brian Eule, Rosabeth Moss Kanter, Phil Pizzo, Michael Balaoing, Laura Geller, Richard Siegel, Jane Lowe, David Morse, Joe Marx, Ai-jen Poo, Barbara Bradley Hagerty, Courtney Martin, Chris Farrell, Mark Miller, Kerry Hannon, Ashton Applewhite, Tim Carpenter, Bill Drayton, and Richard Rothstein. I'd especially like to thank the late Robert Butler and Jack Rosenthal, both of whom were exceptionally kind to me and whose ideas resonated throughout the book's evolution.

I want to express my appreciation for the wonderful family at PublicAffairs and Hachette Book Group, including my editor on this book, Colleen Lawrie, as well as Clive Priddle, Jaime Leifer, Lindsay Fradkoff, and the rest of the team. Susan Weinberg, publisher of the Perseus Book Group, supported this project from the outset. Peter Osnos, a wonderful mentor and good friend over many years, is the person most responsible for me writing books over the past twenty years, period.

In addition, I want to express deep thanks to my colleagues at Encore.org past and present, including Eunice Lin Nichols, Jim

Emerman, Phyllis Segal, Nancy Peterson, Michelle Hynes, Julia Randell-Khan, Aanchal Dhar, Marsha Wooden, Betsy Werley, Megan McCarthy, Marco Austin, Ninia Torrefiel, Ann MacDougall, Duncan Magidson, Aaron Larsen, Aileen Ichikawa, Aireen Navarro Khauv, Cecily Medved, Gary Hume, Corita Brown, Janet Oh, Karimah Nonyameko, Sandy Fernandes, and all who advised and supported me in the writing of the manuscript. Thank to Sarah McKinney, who suggested I read Kareem Abdul-Jabbar's book about his relationship with John Wooden. I'm especially grateful to Encore.org's board of directors for their remarkable support and guidance throughout—in addition to those already named, Sherry Lansing, Susan Gianinno, Ruth Wooden, Dotty Hayes, Webb McKinney, Suzanne Braun Levine, Jaime Magyera, David Vasquez-Levy, and Beverly Ryder.

Deep thanks go to Joyce and Jake Anderson, our neighbors and friends, who have spent so much time with our kids and who have enriched all of our lives. And to Donna Hellenbrand, Lisa Phifer, Rose Nayar, and the whole extended family, who helped to hold down the fort while I was off wrestling with this project.

Finally, I want to thank my immediate family, who put up with all my extended absences, despairing moods, and general distraction for something like a year, or maybe three. This book is dedicated to my wife, Leslie, and our three sons, Gabriel, Levi, and Micah, the little tribe who make life worth living.

NOTES AND SOURCES

For more than three decades, I've been trying to create and promote new roles for older people—roles that use experience to solve important social problems while adding meaning and purpose to longer lives. A particular focus throughout has been opportunities that support and nurture the next generation.

Over that period, I've traveled the country (and some parts of the world) in an attempt to witness promising innovations and conduct in-person interviews with hundreds of individuals directly involved in this work, as well as with a great many thought leaders, activists, and social entrepreneurs toiling in this arena. *How to Live Forever* is my attempt to distill, understand, and integrate what I've seen, heard, and learned.

As such, some chapters in this book draw not only on new material but also on previous research and writing—about mentoring in *The Kindness of Strangers,* about the changing nature of retirement in *Prime Time,* about longer working lives in *Encore,* and about the new map of life in *The Big Shift.* I've likewise drawn extensively from articles and blogs I've written for the *Wall Street Journal, Harvard Business Review,* the *Washington Post, American Prospect,* and other publications.

In some places stories, quotes, and passages from these previously published works appear in this book and are noted below. The notes also list resources that I've drawn upon in this book's chapters and that have influenced my thinking over the years. I hope you'll also review the lists of books, movies, and videos I have enjoyed and highly recommend. You'll find these in the book's appendix.

INTRODUCTION: EXTENSIONS

Two obituaries provide additional details about Gil Stott's life: one from *Princeton Alumni Weekly,* "Memorial: Gil Stott *51," and the other, "Farewell to This Wise, Good Man: Gilmore Stott Dies at Age 91," in the *Swarthmore College Bulletin,* June 2005. In addition, this website was set up to collect remembrances of Stott: http://rememberinggilstott .blogspot.com/.

Kids versus Canes?

For additional information about the more old than young society, see Paul Overberg and Janet Adamy, "Elderly in U.S. Are Projected to Outnumber Children for First Time," *Wall Street Journal,* March 13, 2018; Hansi Lo Wang, "Projections Show an Aging U.S. Population," *NPR Morning Edition,* March 14, 2018; and Becky Gillan, "Top 10 Demographics & Interests Facts About Americans Age 50+," AARP blog, May 14, 2014.

The statistics about young people's status come from a multitude of sources cited in "Our Work: A Framework for Accelerating Progress for Children and Youth in America," America's Promise Alliance, April 2017.

Articles about the Druckenmiller and Canada crusade include Thomas Friedman, "Sorry, Kids. We Ate It All," *New York Times,* October 15, 2013; and Stanley Druckenmiller, Geoffrey Canada, and Kevin Warsh, "Generational Theft Needs to Be Arrested," *Wall Street Journal,* February 14, 2013.

These articles fit into a genre that includes a number of books, among them the following: Laurence J. Kotlikoff and Scott Burns, *The Clash of Generations: Saving Ourselves, Our Kids, and Our Economy* (MIT Press, 2012); Bruce Cannon Gibney, *A Generation of Sociopaths: How the Baby Boomers Betrayed America* (Hachette Books, 2017); and Peter G. Peterson, *Gray Dawn: How the Coming Age Wave Will Transform America—and the World* (Crown, 1999).

Built for Each Other

Recent books on the power of grandparenting include Jane Isay, *Unconditional Love: A Guide to Navigating the Joys and Challenges of Being a Grandparent Today* (Harper, 2018); and Lesley Stahl, *Becoming Grandma: The Joys and Science of the New Grandparenting* (Blue Rider Press, 2016). I've also learned a great deal from the writing of Robin Marantz Henig, including "The Age of Grandparents Is Made of Many Tragedies," *Atlantic*, June 1, 2018.

Sources on the grandmother hypothesis include Judith Shulevitz, "Why Do Grandmothers Exist? Solving an Evolutionary Mystery," *New Republic*, January 28, 2013; Roni Jacobson, "Revisiting the Grandmother Hypothesis: Do Post-menopausal Women Deserve the Credit for Humans' Long Life Span?" *Scienceline*, February 23, 2013; Lindsay Abrams, "The Evolutionary Importance of Grandmothers," *Atlantic*, October 24, 2012; and John Poole, "Why Grandmothers May Hold the Key to Human Evolution," NPR, June 7, 2018.

Laura Carstensen's *A Long, Bright Future: An Action Plan for a Lifetime of Happiness, Health, and Financial Security* (Harmony, 2009) and Alison Gopnik's *The Gardener and the Carpenter: What the New Science of Child Development Tells Us About the Relationship Between Parents and Children* (Farrar, Straus and Giroux, 2016) are a pair of extremely wise books that influenced me deeply.

An essay that influenced my thinking in this section, and throughout the book, is Eric Liu, "How Boomers Left Us With an Ethical Deficit," *Atlantic*, September 24, 2010.

The Ripe Moment

I first told the Cherry Hendrix story in my book *Prime Time: How Baby Boomers Will Revolutionize Retirement and Transform America* (PublicAffairs, 1999). Her obituary in *The Oregonian* recounts Cherry's remarkable life in greater detail: Becca Stanek, "Life Story: Cherry Hendrix, teacher and volunteer," *The Oregonian*, June 24, 2013.

Coming Full Circle

My previous book, *The Big Shift: Navigating the New Stage Beyond Midlife,* was published by PublicAffairs in 2011. It concludes with a chapter on "The Generativity Revolution," which really is a prelude to this book.

Fran Lebowitz's story comes from Terry Gross's interview of John Leland, author of *Happiness Is a Choice You Make: Lessons from a Year Among the Oldest Old* (Sarah Crichton Books, 2018), on NPR's Fresh Air, January 24, 2018.

CHAPTER 1: BIOLOGY FLOWS DOWNHILL

I told a version of this story in my *Wall Street Journal* essay, "How to Add Life to Longer Years," which appeared in the newspaper on May 31, 2015.

Life Extensions

John F. Kennedy's speech, "Special Message to the Congress on the Needs of the Nation's Senior Citizens," was delivered on February 21, 1963. It can be found online, www.presidency.ucsb.edu/ws/?pid=9572, thanks to the American Presidency Project.

Pathways to Encore Purpose, "Purpose in the Encore Years: Shaping Lives of Meaning and Contribution," Stanford Graduate School of Education and Encore.org, 2018, www.encore.org/research/purpose. Also see Jill Suttie, "How to Find Your Purpose in Midlife," *Greater Good Magazine*, March 8, 2018.

Analysis and examples of the immortalists' efforts and how they are portrayed in the media include Tad Friend, "Silicon Valley's Quest to Live Forever," *New Yorker,* April 3, 2017. Also see *Forbes* magazine cover on February 28, 2017, "How to Cheat Death"; *Time* magazine cover on September 20, 2013, "Can Google Solve Death?"; and *Bloomberg* magazine's "Google Wants You to Live Forever," March 9, 2015.

The Gavin Belson parabiosis story is from HBO's "Silicon Valley," www.hbo.com/silicon-valley.

Larry Ellison is quoted in Tyagarajan S, "The Quest to End Death," *Future*, August 31, 2017, https://factordaiiy.com/silicon-valleys-quest -to-end-death/.

Michael Kinsley's rejoinder to Ellison can be found in *Old Age: A Beginner's Guide* (Tim Duggan Books, 2016).

Peter Thiel's quote comes from the foreword to Sonia Arrison, *100+: How the Coming Age of Longevity Will Change Everything, from Careers and Relationships to Family and Faith* (Basic Books, 2011).

Solving the Wrong Problem

Ezekiel Emanuel's quote is from his review, "Tinkers and Tailors: Three Books Look to the Biomedical Frontier," *New York Times*, March 16, 2017. His own plans are described in Ezekiel Emanuel, "Why I Hope to Die at 75," *Atlantic*, October 2014.

Nir Barzilai quoted in Tad Friend, "Silicon Valley's Quest to Live Forever," *New Yorker*, April 3, 2017.

David Ewing Duncan's experiment is described in "How Long Do You Want to Live," *New York Times*, August 25, 2012.

Life's Great Teacher

"World Death Rate Holding Steady at 100 Percent," *The Onion*, January 22, 1997.

Steve Jobs's commencement address can be read or seen on the *Stanford News* website: "'You've Got to Find What You Love,' Jobs Says," June 14, 2015, https://news.stanford.edu/2005/06/14/jobs-061505/.

Biology Flows Downhill

Mitch Albom's relationship with Morrie Schwartz is described in Albom's book *Tuesdays with Morrie: An Old Man, a Young Man, and Life's Greatest Lesson* (Doubleday, 1997).

The description of socioemotional selectivity is from Laura Carstensen's *A Long Bright Future* (Harmony, 2009).

For findings from the Harvard Study of Adult Development, see Robert Waldinger, "What Makes a Good Life? Lessons from the Longest Study on Happiness," TEDxBeaconStreet, November 2015. Also useful are "Can relationships boost longevity and well-being?," *Harvard Health Letter*, June 2017; Liz Mineo, "Good Genes Are Nice, but Joy Is Better," *Harvard Gazette*, April 11, 2017; Colby Itkowitz, "Harvard Researchers Discover the One Thing Everyone Needs for Happier, Healthier Lives," *Washington Post*, March 2, 2016; and Ruth Whippman, "Happiness Is Other People," *New York Times*, October 27, 2017.

Vaillant's research and findings are described in George E. Vaillant, *Aging Well: Surprising Guideposts to a Happier Life from the Landmark Harvard Study of Adult Development* (Little, Brown, 2002); and George E. Vaillant, *Triumphs of Experience: The Men of the Harvard Grant Study* (Belknap Press, 2012).

David Brooks invokes Vaillant's magnificent phrase "biology flows downhill" in "The Geezers' Crusade," *New York Times*, February 1, 2010.

For more about Vaillant's life and work, see Joshua Wolf Shenk, "What Makes Us Happy?" *Atlantic*, June 2009. Shenk describes Vaillant's use of Blake's line, "Joy and woe are woven fine," which I've also invoked in this book.

I Am What Survives of Me

To understand Erik Erikson's views on generativity, see Erik H. Erikson, *Childhood and Society* (W. W. Norton & Co., 1950); Erik H. Erikson, Joan M. Erikson, and Helen Q. Kivnick, *Vital Involvement in Old Age: The Experience of Old Age in Our Time* (W. W. Norton & Co., 1987); and Daniel Goleman, "Erikson, in His Own Old Age, Expands His View of Life," *New York Times*, June 14, 1988.

Other important books on generativity include Dan P. McAdams and Ed De St. Aubin, *Generativity and Adult Development: How and Why We Care for the Next Generation* (American Psychological Association, 1998); John Snarey, *How Fathers Care for the Next*

Generation: A Four-Decade Study (Harvard University Press, 1993); and Bradley Hagerty, *Life Reimagined: The Science, Art, and Opportunity of Midlife* (Riverhead Books, 2016). I am indebted to Professor Gina Lopata Logan of Northwestern's Foley Center for the Study of Lives for taking the time to help me understand the existing state of research on generativity.

Also see Leon R. Kass, "L'Chaim and Its Limits: Why Not Immortality?" in *The Fountain of Youth: Cultural, Scientific, and Ethical Perspectives on a Biomedical Goal*, ed. Stephen G. Post and Robert H. Binstock (Oxford University Press, 2004).

Please note: Some of these ideas were also laid out previously in a blog I coauthored with Trent Stamp for the *Harvard Business Review*, "Aging Societies Should Make More of Mentorship," July 6, 2016.

Living Mortal

Atul Gawande talks about mortality and legacy in *Being Mortal: Medicine and What Matters in the End* (Metropolitan Books, 2014).

The story about the older woman who wanted to take her grandchildren to Disney World comes from Atul Gawande, "What Matters in the End," Transcript from interview with *On Being* host Krista Tippett, October 26, 2017.

For Hall's ideas on life's "Indian summer," see G. Stanley Hall, *Senescence: The Last Half of Life* (D. Appleton, 1922). I described Hall's thinking about both adolescence and the new stage of life between middle age and old age in *The Big Shift*, as well as in the blog, "Sorry, But 60 Is Not the New 40," *Wall Street Journal*, December 9, 2013.

On the question of a perfect age, see Clare Ansberry, "What Is the Perfect Age?," *Wall Street Journal*, January 12, 2018.

The World Is Calling

The Last Word, starring Shirley MacLaine and Amanda Seyfried. Produced by Myriad Pictures, directed by Mark Pellington, 2017.

Creed, starring Sylvester Stallone and Michael B. Jordan. Produced by Metro-Goldwyn-Mayer, directed by Ryan Coogler, 2015.

CHAPTER 2: LOVE AND DEATH
Emmy Werner
Emmy Werner's books, written with Ruth S. Smith, include *Vulnerable Yet Invincible: A Longitudinal Study of Resilient Children and Youth* (McGraw-Hill, 1982); *Overcoming the Odds: High Risk Children from Birth to Adulthood* (Cornell University Press, 1992); and *Journeys from Childhood to Midlife: Risk, Resilience, and Recovery* (Cornell University Press, 2001). I summarized Werner's research and that of the other scholars of resilience in *The Kindness of Strangers: Adult Mentors, Urban Youth, and the New Volunteerism*, revised edition (Cambridge University Press, 1999).

The Big Question
Urie Bronfenbrenner, *The Ecology of Human Development: Experiments by Nature and Design* (Harvard University Press, 1979).

Where Are the Humans?
The Big Brother Big Sister study and findings are analyzed by the researchers who led the work in Jean Baldwin Grossman, Nancy Resch, and Joseph P. Tierney, "Making a Difference: An Impact Study of Big Brothers/Big Sisters (Re-issue of 1995 Study)," IssueLab.org, September 15, 2000.

My book on mentoring looks more broadly at the importance of the subject, as well as the history of this approach to helping young people. See *The Kindness of Strangers: Adult Mentors, Urban Youth, and the New Volunteerism*, revised edition (Cambridge University Press, 1999).

Together with my colleague at Public/Private Ventures, Gary Walker, I attempted to bring together the arguments and research base for expanding mentoring efforts in Gary Walker and Marc Freedman,

"Social Change: One on One: The New Mentoring Movement," *American Prospect*, July–August 1996.

Don't Be Like Me, Every Dollar Spent Twice, and Aggie and Louise
My visits to the Work Connection, Portland's Foster Grandparents Program, and other promising intergenerational initiatives had actually started in the 1980s, alongside my growing interest in mentoring—coming fully into focus after the Big Brothers Big Sisters research.

It is also worth noting that much of the material in these three sections was first presented in my book *Prime Time: How Baby Boomers Will Revolutionize Retirement and Transform America* (PublicAffairs, 1999). In these sections of this book, I returned to the stories of Nick Spanaes, Patsy La Violette, and John Curtis, adapting, distilling, and editing the accounts initially published in *Prime Time*. Likewise, the story of Aggie Bennett and Louise Casey comes from *Prime Time* and is comprised of material published in that book, including both the description of Aggie and Louise's work at Maine Medical Center and first person narratives from them. I attempted to blend these elements together in Chapter 2 to bring their stories to life. I also returned to the Portland Foster Grandparent program in the summer of 2017 to once again visit Maine Medical Center and to interview the director of the Foster Grandparent program today, Susan Lavigne. Susan knew and worked with Aggie and Louise, Patsy Violette, and John Curtis, all of whom have since passed away. I should also note that I wrote about Aggie and Louise in the essay "Don't Leave a Legacy; Live One," *Harvard Business Review*, December 11, 2012.

CHAPTER 3: AGE APARTHEID
Information about Big Ben Schleifer and Youngtown comes from multiple sources, primary among them collections housed in the Youngtown Historical Society in Peoria, Arizona. Particularly helpful was a powerpoint on the history of Youngtown prepared by Heidi Speed, who runs the society and is Youngtown's librarian. I also benefitted from Joseph Stocker's "The Story of BIG BEN," an essay in the fifth anniversary of

Youngtown publication, as well as from interviews with individuals involved in the Chaz Cope case, including former Arizona state attorney general Grant Woods. In addition, I spent time at the Sun City Historical Society. I first wrote about both Youngtown and Sun City in *Prime Time* but revisited the story and influence of these communities in this book.

I'm deeply indebted, particularly, to Andrew D. Blechman's superb history of age-segregated retirement communities, including Youngtown and Sun City, *Leisureville: Adventures in a World Without Children* (Atlantic Monthly Press, 2008). A number of the quotes from Ben Schleifer (including "Our first obligation when I was a boy . . ."), as well as details of the Chaz Cope story, are drawn from Blechman's meticulously researched book. Also worth reading is his op-ed on age segregation: Andrew D. Blechman, "Left out of 'leisureville': Fast-growing retirement communities legally practice age discrimination," *Los Angeles Times*, July 8, 2008.

Other invaluable resources on age-segregated retirement communities, including Sun City, are Francis FitzGerald's *Cities on a Hill: A Journey Through Contemporary American Cultures* (Simon and Schuster, 1987) and Deane Simpson's *Young-Old: Urban Utopias of an Aging Society* (Lars Muller, 2015). Also worth reading is the *Time* magazine cover story about Del Webb and Sun City that appeared on August 3, 1962, entitled, "The Retirement City: A New Way of Life for the Old."

Too Old to Work, Too Young to Die
I devoted considerable attention to the history of old age in America in *Prime Time*, including a survey of research on the Puritans' views of aging and intergenerational relations. I likewise traced the development of Social Security and the invention of the golden years in that book. This section, and much of Chapter 3, is based on that earlier account. Particularly valuable resources on the subject include W. Andrew Achenbaum, *Old Age in a New Land: The American Experience Since 1790* (Johns Hopkins University Press, 1978); W. Andrew Achenbaum, "What Is Retirement For?" *Wilson Quarterly*, Spring 2006; Thomas R. Cole, *The Journey of Life: A Cultural History of Aging*

in America (Cambridge University Press, 1991); Dora Costa, *The Evolution of Retirement: An American Economic History, 1880–1990* (University of Chicago Press, 1998); David J. Ekerdt, "Retirement," in *The Encyclopedia of Aging*, fourth edition, ed. George Maddox (Springer Publishing Company, 2006); David Hackett Fischer, *Growing Old in America* (Oxford University Press, 1979); and William Graebner, *A History of Retirement: The Meaning and Function of an American Institution, 1885–1978* (Yale University Press, 1980).

One of the great pleasures of the research for this book was discovering Howard Chudacoff's *How Old Are You? Age Consciousness in American Culture* (Princeton University Press, 1989). Chudacoff's quote in this section comes from that book. This section's account of how we became segregated by age is also indebted to the superb essay by historian Steven Mintz, "Generations Divided: How America Became Segregated by Age," *Psychology Today*, February 21, 2015; and Mintz's fine book, *The Prime of Life: A History of Modern Adulthood* (Belknap Press, an imprint of Harvard University Press, 2015).

I also want to direct readers to a superb distillation of the research and implications of age segregation, Leon Neyfakh's "What 'Age Segregation' Does to America," *Boston Globe*, August 31, 2014. Neyfakh's essay opened my eyes to the history of age segregation. A number of the sources cited in this chapter came from reading Neyfakh's review. Finally, I drew in this section on Generations United and the Eisner Foundation's timely report, "I Need You, You Need Me: The Young, the Old, and What We Can Achieve Together," May 2017.

One additional note: I wrote about the impact of age segregation for *Harvard Business Review* (with Trent Stamp of the Eisner Foundation), adapting material presented in this chapter (as well as in Chapter 5) of this book. See Marc Freedman and Trent Stamp, "The U.S. Isn't Just Getting Older, It's Getting More Segregated by Age," June 6, 2018, as well as a related essay published shortly after the *HBR* piece: Marc Freedman and Trent Stamp, "Can the Fight Against Age Segregation Unite Us?," *Next Avenue*, June 21, 2018.

Material on Walter Reuther comes from Nelson Lichtenstein, *The Most Dangerous Man in Detroit* (University of Illinois Press, 1997).

Not Segregation, Integration

This section draws heavily on Lewis Mumford, "For Older People—Not Segregation But Integration," *Architectural Digest*, May 1956.

Inventing the Golden Years

I wrote extensively about Webb and Sun City in *Prime Time* and also in the *Washington Post*'s Outlook section, "No Country for Old People?" January 27, 2008. The material presented here is largely adapted from that book and essay. Those earlier accounts provide more detailed information about Webb, Sun City, and their influence on the changing nature of retirement in America.

Making the Natural Unnatural

See FitzGerald's *Cities on a Hill* for her observations about the absence of children at communities like Sun City.

In addition to *Leisureville*, the Chaz Cope situation was well covered by the *New York Times*. In this section I drew upon these sources, my earlier descriptions of the incident in *Prime Time*, and new material gathered from Youngtown's Historical Society and from interviews with Grant Woods and others.

The *New York Times* coverage of Sun City's age police is contained in "In Haven for Over-55 Set, Age Police Hunt Violators Who Shriek or Toddle," August 28, 2010.

Swimming Upstream

As noted above, important insights about the nature and problems of age segregation can be found in Leon Neyfakh's "What 'Age Segregation' Does to America" (*Boston Globe*, August 31, 2014), which describes Winkler's research and her perspective on these findings. More details from her study can be found in Richelle Winkler,

"Segregated by Age: Are We Becoming More Divided?" *Population Research and Policy Review* 32, no 5 (2013): 717–727. Other quotes and references come from "Housing Trends Update for the 55+ Market," MetLife Mature Market Institute and the National Association of Home Builders, January 2011; and Suzanne Gerber, "The Love Advice That Shocked Expert Karl Pillemer," *Huffington Post,* December 6, 2017.

Ben Sasse's book is called *The Vanishing American Adult: Our Coming-of-Age Crisis—and How to Rebuild a Culture of Self-Reliance* (St. Martin's Press, 2017) and contains a chapter on the perils of age segregation.

Additional articles on age segregation and its impact include Peter Uhlenberg and Jenny De Jong Gierveld, "Age-segregation in later life: an examination of personal networks," *Aging & Society* 24, no 1 (January 2004): 5–28; Ashton Applewhite, "You're How Old? We'll Be in Touch," *New York Times,* September 3, 2016; and Gunhild O. Hagestad and Peter Uhlenberg, "The Social Separation of Old and Young: A Root of Ageism," *Journal of Social Issues* 61, no. 2 (2005): 343–360.

On the connection to loneliness, see Vivek Murthy, "Work and the Loneliness Epidemic," *Harvard Business Review,* Septemper 28, 2017; Eric Klinenberg, "Is Loneliness a Health Epidemic?" *New York Times,* February 9, 2018; Rhitu Chatterjee, "Americans Are a Lonely Lot, and Young People Bear the Heaviest Burden," NPR, May 1, 2018.

John Prine's "Hello in There" originally appeared on his album called *John Prine,* released by Atlantic Records in 1971.

I first wrote about my father's experience in a blog for the *Wall Street Journal,* "Why Eldercare and Child-Care Facilities Should Be in the Same Place," November 27, 2016. This section is adapted from that earlier essay.

CHAPTER 4: AN ARMY FOR YOUTH

I wrote about my experience driving with John Gardner for the *Wall Street Journal's* Experts section, "Why John Gardner Is My Retirement

Role Model," April 4, 2014, and also described my relationship with Gardner in *Prime Time*. This opening section of Chapter 4, as well as the closing paragraphs of the chapter (describing the final time I heard Gardner speak publicly), are adapted from that *Wall Street Journal* essay. The story about meeting Gardner at the Carnegie conference initially appeared in *Prime Time*. It is presented again here in a lightly edited form.

Also see Gardner's book *No Easy Victories*, published in 1968, which includes the essay "On Aging," as well as his speech on self-renewal to McKinsey. For an account of that speech and a link to it, see Bill Taylor, "The Best Leaders are Insatiable Learners," *Harvard Business Review*, September 4, 2014. And worth reading is Gardner, *Self-Renewal: The Individual and the Innovative Society* (W. W. Norton, 1963).

Experience Corps

I have told the story of Experience Corps's origins in *Prime Time* and in multiple articles since that time. Elements are also described in Robert Putnam and Lew Feldstein, *Better Together: Restoring the American Community* (Simon & Schuster, 2003), which contains a chapter on Experience Corps.

The strong fit between older people and national service opportunities is described in Richard Danzig and Peter Szanton, *National Service: What Would It Mean?* (Lexington Books, 1986).

Gardner's concept paper on Experience Corps was published as a column in AARP's magazine back when it was called *Modern Maturity*. You can now find it online as an appendix to "Scientific Method in the Real World: Experience Corps and the Johns Hopkins Study," May 2014.

Research from Johns Hopkins and Washington University on the impact of Experience Corps on students and corps members can be found at www.aarp.org/experience-corps/our-impact/experience -corps-research-studies/. Dr. Linda Fried has written extensively about the benefits and lessons of Experience Corps, including in a seminal article for *Atlantic*, "Making Aging Positive," June 1, 2014. Also, Jack Rowe, Linda Fried, and Dawn Carr describe the program's benefits in "Productivity & Engagement in an Aging America: The Role of Volunteerism," *Daedalus*, April 2015.

Beyond the Numbers

The section laying out the changing context of African American neighborhoods and why that matters for efforts like Experience Corps and mentoring more broadly, draws on research and writing I initially presented in *The Kindness of Strangers*. It is included here in an updated and distilled form. William Julius Wilson's research is contained initially in his classic book, *The Declining Significance of Race: Blacks and Changing American Institutions* (University of Chicago Press, 1978). Elijah Anderson's findings are described in *Streetwise: Race, Class, and Change in an Urban Community* (University of Chicago Press, 1993).

Colin Powell's reflections are included in "Colin Powell: Who Mentored You?," Harvard T. H. Chan School of Public Health, https://sites.sph.harvard.edu/wmy/celebrities/colin-powell/, as well as Monte Whaley, "Powell gives kids a 4-star message," *Denver Post*, July 13, 2000. See also Colin Powell, *My American Journey* (Random House, 1995).

The stories of and quotes from Harold Allen, Martha Jones, and others at Taylor Elementary School all come from my book *Prime Time* and are distilled and adapted here.

Rob Gurwitt's essay on Experience Corps was published in the Innovations series, by Civic Ventures (now called Encore.org). This series is out of print and not available online.

Breathtaking Opportunities

For a comprehensive account of Gardner's life and career see www.pbs.org/johngardner/, part of the project *John Gardner: Uncommon*

American. See also Robert D. McFadden, "John W. Gardner, 89, Founder of Common Cause and Adviser to Presidents, Dies," *The New York Times,* February 18, 2002. The story about Gardner's mother comes from his speech at the twentieth anniversary of Common Cause, delivered on September 15, 1990, in Washington, DC. I wrote about Gardner's final speech, as stated earlier, in the *Wall Street Journal* essay "Why John Gardner Is My Retirement Role Model." The full text of the speech, delivered at the Coming of Age Conference at the Miyako Hotel in San Francisco on October 5, 2000, is unpublished. In this section I also drew upon a conversation with John Gardner's grandson, Gardner Trimble.

CHAPTER 5: DREAMING AND SCHEMING

My sources on Maggie Kuhn, founder of the Gray Panthers, range from her autobiography to media clips to an interview with Nancy Henkin in 2017 and include Maggie Kuhn, *No Stone Unturned: The Life and Times of Maggie Kuhn* (Ballantine Books, 1991); Ken Dychtwald, "Remembering Maggie Kuhn: Gray Panthers Founder on the 5 Myths of Aging," conducted in 1978, posted on Huffington Post, May 31, 2012; and Judy Klemesrud, "Gray Panther Founder and a Family of Choice," *New York Times,* June 22, 1981.

Kuhn's quotes on age segregation are drawn from the highly recommended and extremely thoughtful interview with her by Ken Dychtwald, contained in the *Huffington Post* article listed above. The interview provides a window into Kuhn's thinking on an array of important topics.

Interviews with Nancy Henkin were conducted in person and by phone in January 2018 and add to our conversations over more than two decades. On a related note, the Intergenerational Center at Temple University, founded by Henkin, was a leading center of intergenerational thought and innovation. Under her leadership, the center developed a wide range of critical intergenerational programs, including ones that focused on mentoring, family support, and cross-age relationships in immigrant and refugee communities. The center's recent closure after thirty-six years is a loss to the cause of bringing generations together for mutual benefit.

The Innovation Imperative

For more about breakthrough innovations in aging of the past half century and their considerable benefits, see Patrick J. Kigger, "Ethel Percy Andrus: AARP Founder Proved There's Strength in Numbers," www.aarp.org/politics-society/history/champions-of-aging-photos /ethel-percy-andrus-aarp-founder.html; C. Eugene Steuerle, "Social Security and the Poor," Urban Institute, December 23, 2000; and "Who's Poor in America? 50 Years into the 'War on Poverty,' a Data Portrait," Pew Research Center, January 13, 2014.

The Thomas Mann quote comes from *Doctor Faustus: The Life of the German Composer Adrian Leverkuhn As Told by a Friend* (Everyman's Library, 1858).

The Inventors

Information about Treehouse comes from a visit to the program, including interviews with Judy Cockerton, Treehouse staff, and numerous residents. In addition, I collected information from a variety of sources, including a profile and video on Judy Cockerton, when she won the Purpose Prize in 2012, https://encore.org/purpose-prize /judy-cockerton/; "In Easthampton Village, Everyone Helps the Children," *Boston Globe,* December 21, 2015; and "Rebuilding Foster Care from the Ground Up," Innovation Hub from WGBH and PRI, August 25, 2017. Sources on Hope Meadows include a documentary portrait completed by Rob Gurwitt and Alex Harris, now out of print; a profile on Brenda Eheart when she was named a Purpose Prize Fellow in 2009, https://encore.org/purpose-prize/brenda-krause -eheart-2/; Wes Smith, *Hope Meadows: Real Life Stories of Healing and Caring from an Inspiring Community* (Berkley Hardcover, 2001); and Ina Jaffe, "A \ Built Around Older Adults Caring for Adoptive Families," NPR Morning Edition, August 4, 2015.

For information on new efforts from social innovators and corporations to age-integrate housing, see "Skyler: A New Aging Tower," Hollwich Kushner, https://hwkn.com/projects/skyler/; Matthias Hollwich, *New Aging: Live Smarter Now to Live Better Forever* (Penguin Books, 2016); Jesse Dorris, "Hollwich Kushner Announces Skyler, a Prototype for Multigenerational Living," *Interior Design,* April 8, 2016; Bill Thomas, "The First Minka House," Changing Aging newsletter, August 1, 2017; "Minka: Age-Friendly Dwellings, Tools and Services," Minka, https://myminka.com; Bob Tedeschi, "A Physician Homebuilder Tries to Upend the Nursing Home Industry—and Give Seniors Back Their Independence," *STAT,* January 4, 2018: "NextGen: The Home Within a Home," Lennar, www.lennar.com/nextgen; and "GenSmart Suite, Multigenerational Home Solution," Pardee Homes, www.pardeehomes.com/trends-and-design/gensmart-smart-solution-for-multigenerational-living/.

The Integrators

I visited Judson Manor in November 2017 and had the pleasure of interviewing residents, including artists in residence, and administrators. The quotes from Laura Berick and Tiffany Tieu come from "A Retirement Home for Young and Old," Great Big Story (video), September 11, 2016—and the story about Tieu's dog comes from a conversation with Laura Berick. Additional sources include John Hanc, "In Cleveland, Young and Old Keep Tempo of Life," *New York Times,* May 13, 2015; Steve Hartman, "Making Beautiful Music in a Cleveland Retirement Community," CBS Evening News, October 14, 2014; and "Resident Throws Wedding Reception for Former Artist-in-Residence," Judson Smart Living Blog, October 15, 2014. Additional articles about Judson's program can be found at www.judsonsmartliving.org/about/intergenerational-programs/.

On cohousing, see Chris Bentley, "Can Boomers Make Cohousing Mainstream?" CityLab.com, January 20, 2015.

I interviewed Nesterly's cofounders, Noelle Marcus and Rachel Goor, by phone. Additional sources on Nesterly include Linda Poon,

"Helping Boomers Find Millennial Roommates," CityLab.com, July 1, 2017; Madeline Bilis, "This Housing App Pairs Boston's Baby Boomers with Graduate Student Roommates," *Boston Magazine*, January 2, 2018; Kaya Laterman, "Getting a Roommate in Your Golden Years," *New York Times*, January 12, 2018.

I visited Gorham House in the summer of 2017, conducting interviews and watching the program in action. For more information about the preschool and its role in Gorham House, visit www.gorham-house.com/pre-school/. See also Julie Pike's article "Intergenerational Connections at Gorham House," *Free Press*, April 16, 2018; and Bill Gillis's obituary in the *Sun Journal*, January 27, 2017.

I visited Rainbow Intergenerational Learning Center and Child Care in 2017. I wrote about Rainbow previously in *Prime Time*. The program was also the subject of a photo essay commissioned by Encore.org (then Civic Ventures) by Rob Gurwitt and Alex Harris. That essay, no longer in print, contains a history of the Learning Center.

The interview with Donna Butts was conducted by phone in 2018. The quote comes from Generations United, "All in Together: Creating Places Where Young and Old Thrive," June 2018. Also see Julie Halpert, "Fostering Connections Beetween Young and Old: A new report on intergenerational programs calls for shared spaces to help combat isolation among the elderly," *New York Times*, June 5, 2018.

The Infiltrators

I met with and reported on Encore Fellow James Otieno for *The Big Shift*. You can read the text of his comments in the book's appendix. See also Mike Cassidy, "Second Careers That Give Back," *Mercury News*, November 1, 2009; and *The Intern*, starring Robert De Niro and Anne Hathaway, released by Warner Bros. Pictures, directed by Nancy Meyers, 2015.

I taught a class at the University of Minnesota's Advanced Careers program in fall 2017. See also Douglas Belkin, "Baby Boomers Looking for Reinvention Try College—Again," *Wall Street Journal*, December 28, 2017.

Nancy Morrow-Howell and the Harvey A. Friedman Center for Aging, "Washington University's Response to Population Aging: Creating a University for Life," January 10, 2018. I wrote about the idea of a new stage of education for *HBR*: "Universities Cater to a New Demographic: Boomers," *Harvard Business Review*, August 22, 2014.

Pumping Up the Volume

On China's population, see Joseph F. Coughlin's article "China's Gray Revolution: Why China May Invent the New Business of Aging," BigThink.com, undated.

The final quote in this chapter from Bill Thomas can be found in Tiffany R. Jansen's article "The Preschool Inside a Nursing Home," *Atlantic*, January 20, 2016.

CHAPTER 6: A VILLAGE FOR ALL AGES

My guide to St. Joseph's, St. John's-St. Margaret's, and all the aspects of Singapore's plan was Dr. Leng Leng Thang, professor at the National University of Singapore and author of the book *Generations in Touch: Linking the Old and Young in a Tokyo Neighborhood* (Cornell University Press, 2001). I spent a week in Singapore during September of 2017, conducting numerous interviews with officials, academics, and participants in the nation's ambitious aging plan.

A description of St. Joseph's intergenerational efforts is contained in multiple news articles, including Liyana Othman, "St. Joseph's Home Opens Childcare Centre, Intergenerational Playground in Nursing Home," Channel NewsAsia, August 28, 2017; "Singapore gets its first child care centre in a nursing home," YoungParents.com /sg, August 30, 2017; and Dr. Amy Khor, senior minister of state for health, speech at the official opening and fortieth-anniversary celebration of St. Joseph's Home, March 19, 2018. For more on the Happy Coffins project, check out the Lien Foundation website, lienfoundation.org, and lifebeforedeath.com/happy-coffins.

Around the World

Lucy Kellaway first wrote about Now Teach in the *Financial Times*, "I'm Leaving and I Want You to Join Me," November 20, 2016. You can read her occasional missives from the classroom here: www.ft.com/comment/lucy-kellaway. Also see Will Hazell, "'The Most Difficult Thing Is the Total Loss of Control': Meet the Now Teach Career Switchers," October 27, 2017; and "'Teaching Is Brutal': Now Teach Founder Reflects on Her First Months in the Classroom," November 20, 2017. Both can be found at Tes.com.

Dr. Amy Khor's quote comes from Janice Heng, "$3 billion Action Plan for Successful Ageing launched to help seniors age well," *Straits Times*, February 24, 2016. The Singapore plan is contained in a master document, online at www.moh.gov.sg. Also see Tara Bahrampour's article "What Singapore's Plan for an Aging Population Can Teach the United States," *Washington Post*, November 2, 2015.

The Circle of Life

Project Spring-Winter (psw.sjsm.org.sg) is described on the St. John's-St. Margaret's website (www.sjsm.org.sg) and in this news article: Kelly Ng, "Church Pioneers Integrated Facility for Children, Seniors," TODAYOnline, May 13, 2018. For information about *The Growing Season* and Providence Mount St. Vincent's Intergenerational Learning Center see Tiffany R. Jansen, "The Preschool Inside a Nursing Home," *Atlantic*, January 20, 2016.

Comprehensive Action

I first wrote about Kennedy's speech in *Prime Time*, charting his plans for engaging the older population in service projects, as well as other efforts from the early 1960s aimed at that goal. The passages here draw heavily on my earlier writing. Information about these plans is in President John F. Kennedy's speech on February 21, 1963, "Special Message to the Congress on the Needs of the Nation's Senior Citizens." I also conducted numerous historical interviews over many years with individuals engaged in these efforts, including Sargent Shriver and John Gardner, and reviewed extensive congressional testimony by Robert F. Kennedy, John Gardner, Willard Wirtz, and others.

London Calling

As mentioned, Lucy Kellaway has written about her experience and that of the other Now Teach educators in a procession of pieces in the *Financial Times*, including "Could Do Better: My First Half Term as a Maths Teacher," October 18, 2017; and "Teaching Is Bending Us out of Shape—in a Good Way," April 8, 2018. Kellaway's TEDx talk on the program ("I'm Becoming a Teacher at 58—This Is Why You Should Too," July 17, 2017) is also worth viewing. The figures about new teachers over fifty come from Kellaway's articles.

Other media about Now Teach includes Lisa O'Kelly, "I'm Getting a Big Buzz out of It: Five Former Professionals on Their First Term Teaching," *Guardian*, March 11, 2018; Claire Jones, "Why High-Flying Professionals Choose to Be Teachers," BBC News, December 22, 2017; and "A Plan to Turn High-Flying Oldies into Teachers," *Economist*, November 24, 2016.

The quotes from Chris Forsyth come from an interview with him during a visit to Ark Putney Academy, and from Lucy Kellaway's article "Why we went back to school," *Financial Times*, August 31, 2017. The long quote from Kellaway is from her column, "Could do better," in the *Financial Times*.

Betty Friedan's phrase—"the youth short-circuit"—is from her book *The Fountain of Age* (Touchstone, 1993).

CHAPTER 7: REROUTING THE RIVER OF LIFE

Matt Baume, "Bay Area Cities Rediscover the Creeks Under Their Streets," StreetsBlog, April 9, 2010.

For Jo Ann Jenkins's views on the need to transform the culture and institutions of later life, see *Disrupt Aging: A Bold New Path To Living Your Best Life at Every Age* (PublicAffairs, 2016).

More information about the Eisner Foundation's work can be found in Alyssa Ochs and David Callahan, "Intergenerational Funding: What This Foundation is Doing to Bring Children and Seniors Together," December 15, 2016, as well as on the foundation's website, www.eisnerfoundation.org.

Forging Ahead

I wrote about this history of mentoring in *The Kindness of Strangers*.

Rabbi Lord Jonathan Sacks writes about Moses ("To 120: Growing Old, Staying Young," August 8, 2016) and on Now Teach ("The More You Give, the More You'll Be Given," November 25, 2016) on his blog (RabbiSacks.org).

Marci Alboher's *New York Times* column is "If You Don't Have Children, What Do You Leave Behind," February 27, 2018.

Thomas Friedman, "From Hands to Heads to Hearts," *New York Times*, January 3, 2017. The interview with Bill Gates is in *Quartz*, "Bill Gates: The Robot That Takes Your Job Should Pay Taxes," February 17, 2017. Also see Geoff Colvin's *Humans Are Underrated: What High Achievers Know That Brilliant Machines Never Will* (Portfolio/Penguin, 2015).

Bryan Stevenson's counsel is in his book *Just Mercy: A Story of Justice and Redemption* (Spiegel & Grau, 2014), as well as in his TED talk, "We Need to Talk About Injustice," March 5, 2012.

See Alison Gopnik's *The Gardener and the Carpenter: What the New Science of Child Development Tells Us About the Relationship Between Parents and Children* (Farrar, Straus and Giroux, 2016).

I told this story about Aggie Bennett and Susan originally in *Prime Time*. The quotes from Aggie included here come from that book.

From Generation to Generation

For more information about Generation to Generation, see iamgen-2gen.org.

Articles describing the campaign and its components include Sandra Block, "Finding an Encore with Meaning," *Chicago Tribune*,

January 26, 2018; Nancy Collamer, "Meet the Encore Prize Winners Championing Youth," Next Avenue, October 18, 2017; Richard Eisenberg, "How to Stand Up and Show Up for America's Kids," Next Avenue, November 17, 2016; and Paul Taylor, "A Generation Gives Back," *AARP Bulletin*, November 2016.

CHAPTER 8: LIVING MORTAL

The film *Keep On Keepin' On*, winner of the 2014 audience award at the Tribeca Film Festival, was directed by Alan Hicks. Much of the information in this section comes from the film, and from a 2018 interview with Justin Kauflin (more information on Kauflin can be found at www.justinkauflin.com).

Other articles about the film and the Terry-Kauflin relationship include Tad Friend, "Protégé," *New Yorker*, November 3, 2014; Clark Terry's obituary in the *New York Times*, February 22, 2015; and "Something in Common with His Mentor," September 26, 2014, the *New York Times'* review of the film. Also worth reading: *Clark: The Autobiography of Clark Terry* (University of California Press, 2011).

How to Live Mortal sections

David Brooks discusses eulogy virtues in his TED talk, "Should You Live for Your Résumé . . . or Your Eulogy?" April 14, 2014; in his *New York Times* column "The Moral Bucket List," April 25, 2015; and in his book *The Road to Character* (Random House, 2015).

Carl Jung's views about the afternoon of life are contained in "The Stages of Life," in *The Collected Works of C. G. Jung*, volume 8 (Princeton University Press, 1960).

Chip Conley's ideas are in the book *Wisdom@Work*, as well as at www.chipconley.com; and "I Joined Airbnb and Here's What I Learned About Age, Wisdom, and the Tech Industry," *Harvard Business Review*, April 18, 2017.

Courtney Martin's relationship with Louise Dunlap is described in her blog for *On Being* (https://onbeing.org/author/courtneymartin).

Also see her book *The New Better Off: Reinventing the New American Dream* (Seal Press, 2016).

For information on the importance of relationships for young people, see "Don't Quit on Me: What Young People Who Left School Say About the Power of Relationships," America's Promise Alliance, September 6, 2015.

The Rosalind Guttman / Spencer Sleyon bond is described in Daniel Victor, "He's 22. She's 81. Their Friendship Is Melting Hearts," *New York Times*, December 6, 2017, as well as in Allison Klein, "A Rapper and an 81-Year-Old Just Met in Person after Bonding over Words with Friends for More Than a Year," *Washington Post*, December 4, 2017.

Karen Sughrue's story about her volunteer work with Strive for College can be found at http://generationtogeneration.org/stories /karen-sughrue.

For Pausch's advice see Randy Pausch, *The Last Lecture* (Hyperion, 2008).

For the Hal Garman story, see Paul Taylor's article "A Generation Gives Back," *AARP Bulletin*, November 2016.

Table Wisdom's story can be found at www.generationtogeneration .org/2017-encore-prize-table-wisdom.

Michelle Kuo's beautiful meditation is from *Reading with Patrick: A Teacher, a Student, and a Life-Changing Friendship* (Random House, 2017).

I told the EnCorps Teacher Program story, "Need STEM Teachers? Look to Older Adults," in my blog for the *Wall Street Journal*, April 22, 2018. The section of on Baltazar Villalba is adapted from that piece.

Coming Home

Kareem Abdul-Jabbar tells the story of his relationship with John Wooden in *Coach Wooden and Me: Our 50-Year Friendship On and Off the Court* (Grand Central Publishing, 2017). Also informative are interviews with Abdul-Jabbar and articles prompted by his book. All quotes in this section are either from *Coach Wooden and Me* or from the following sources (I did not interview Kareem Abdul-Jabbar): Mike McPhate, "California Today: Kareem Abdul-Jabbar on the Wisdom of John Wooden," *New York Times*, June 1, 2017; Mike James, "Kareem Abdul-Jabbar Memorializes the Great John Wooden in 'Coach Wooden and Me,'" *Los Angeles Times*, June 22, 2017; Ed Sherman, "Kareem Abdul-Jabbar Discusses His New Memoir, 'Coach Wooden and Me,'" *Chicago Tribune*, June 6, 2017; and Bill Littlefield, "50 Years of Coach Wooden and Kareem, Through Racism, Olympic Boycotts and More," WBUR, May 19, 2017.

Wendy Oxenhorn's quote comes from Tad Friend's *New Yorker* article, "The Protégé."

EPILOGUE: WE WAIT TOO LONG

The Hyowon Healing Center is described in multiple articles and videos, including Choe Sang-Hun, "South Koreans, Seeking New Zest for Life, Experience Their Own Funerals," *New York Times*, Oct. 26, 2016; as well as in "In Seoul, Preventing Suicide by Simulating Death," *Atlantic*, video, May 6, 2016; and Jamie Gumbrecht, "People Attend Their Own Funerals to Improve Their Lives," *CNN*, December 13, 2015. My description is based entirely on these secondary sources.

The *Philadelphia Daily News* article on my father, Bernard Freedman, is by Drew McQuade, "You Can Bank on His Presence at the Vaults," *Philadelphia Daily News*, April 22, 1993.

Prayers come from "A Jewish Service During Shiva," Association for Progressive Judaism, http://projudaism.org/wp-content/uploads/2014/12/Shiva-Service-3.pdf.

RECOMMENDED READING LIST

Abdul-Jabbar, Kareem. *Coach Wooden and Me: Our 50-Year Friendship On and Off the Court.* Grand Central Publishing, 2017.

Agronin, Marc E. *The End of Old Age: Living a Longer, More Purposeful Life.* Da Capo Lifelong Books, 2018.

Alboher, Marci. *The Encore Career Handbook. How to Make a Living and a Difference in the Second Half of Life.* Workman Publishing Company, 2013.

Albom, Mitch. *Tuesdays With Morrie: An Old Man, a Young Man, and Life's Greatest Lesson.* Doubleday, 1997.

Applewhite, Ashton. *This Chair Rocks: A Manifesto Against Ageism.* Networked Books, 2016.

Aronson, Louise. *Elderhood: Redefining Aging, Transforming Medicine, Reimagining Life.* Bloomsbury Publishing, 2019.

Blechman, Andrew D. *Leisureville: Adventures in a World Without Children.* Atlantic Monthly Press, 2008.

Brooks, David. *The Road to Character.* Random House, 2015.

Brooks, David. *The Second Mountain: The Quest for a Moral Life.* Random House, 2019.

Butler, Robert N. *Why Survive? Being Old in America.* Harper & Row, 1975.

Carstensen, Laura. *A Long Bright Future: An Action Plan for a Lifetime of Happiness, Health, and Financial Security.* Harmony, 2009.

Chudacoff, Howard. *How Old Are You? Age Consciousness in American Culture.* Princeton University Press, 1989.

Conley, Chip. *Wisdom at Work: The Making of a Modern Elder.* Currency, 2018.

Coughlin, Joseph F. *The Longevity Economy: Unlocking the World's Fastest-Growing, Most Misunderstood Market.* PublicAffairs, 2017.

Denworth, Lydia. *Friendship: The Evolution, Biology, and Extraordinary Power of Life's Fundamental Bond.* W.W. Norton & Company, 2020.

Dychtwald, Ken, and Joe Flower. *Age Wave: How the Most Important Trend of Our Time Will Change Your Future.* Bantam, 1990.

Dychtwald, Ken, and Daniel Kadlec. *A New Purpose: Redefining Money, Family, Work, Retirement, and Success.* William Morrow, 2010.

Friedan, Betty. *The Fountain of Age.* Touchstone, 1993.

Friedman, Thomas. *Thank You for Being Late: An Optimist's Guide to Thriving in the Age of Accelerations*. Farrar, Straus and Giroux, 2016.

Gardner, John W. *Self-Renewal: The Individual and the Innovative Society*. W. W. Norton, 1963.

Gawande, Atul. *Being Mortal: Medicine and What Matters in the End*. Metropolitan Books, 2014.

Gratton, Lynda, and Andrew Scott. *The 100-Year Life: Living and Working in an Age of Longevity*. Bloomsbury, 2016.

Gopnik, Alison. *The Gardener and the Carpenter: What the New Science of Child Development Tells Us About the Relationship Between Parents and Children*. Farrar, Straus and Giroux, 2016.

Hagerty, Barbara Bradley. *Life Reimagined: The Science, Art, and Opportunity of Midlife*. Riverhead Books, 2016.

Hannon, Kerry. *Great Jobs for Everyone 50+, Updated Edition: Finding Work That Keeps You Happy and Healthy . . . and Pays the Bills*. Wiley, 2017.

Harris, Nadine Burke. *The Deepest Well: Healing the Long-Term Effects of Childhood Adversity*. Houghton Mifflin Harcourt, 2018.

Heimans, Jeremy, and Henry Timms. *New Power: How Power Works in Our Hyperconnected World—and How to Make It Work for You*. Doubleday, 2018.

Hollwich, Matthias, and Bruce Mau Design. *New Aging: Live Smarter Now to Live Better Forever*. Penguin Books, 2016.

Irving, Paul. *The Upside of Aging: How Long Life Is Changing the World of Health, Work, Innovation, Policy and Purpose*. Wiley, 2014.

Isay, Jane. *Unconditional Love: A Guide to Navigating the Joys and Challenges of Being a Grandparent Today*. Harper, 2018.

Jenkins, Jo Ann. *Disrupt Aging: A Bold New Path to Living Your Best Life at Every Age*. PublicAffairs, 2016.

Kinsley, Michael. *Old Age: A Beginner's Guide*. Tim Duggan Books, 2016.

Kirp, David. *Kids First: Five Big Ideas for Transforming Children's Lives and America's Future*. PublicAffairs, 2011.

Leland, John. *Happiness Is a Choice You Make: Lessons from a Year Among the Oldest Old*. Sarah Crichton Books, 2018.

Liu, Eric. *Guiding Lights: How to Mentor—and Find Life's Purpose*. Ballantine Books, 2006.

Martin, Courtney E. *The New Better Off: Reinventing the American Dream*. Seal Press, 2016.

Miller, Mark. *Jolt: Stories of Trauma and Transformation*. Post Hill Press, 2018.

Moen, Phyllis. *Encore Adulthood: Boomers on the Edge of Risk, Renewal, and Purpose*. Oxford, 2016.

Murthy, Vivek. *Together: The Healing Power of Human Connection in a Sometimes Lonely World.* Harper Wave, 2020.

Pinker, Susan. *The Village Effect: How Face-to-Face Contact Can Make Us Healthier, Happier, and Smarter.* Spiegel & Grau, 2014.

Poo, Ai-jen. *The Age of Dignity: Preparing for the Elder Boom in a Changing America.* New Press, 2015.

Putnam, Robert D. *Our Kids: The American Dream in Crisis.* Simon & Schuster, 2015.

Putnam, Robert D., and Lewis M. Feldstein. *Better Together: Restoring the American Community.* Simon & Schuster, 2003.

Rauch, Jonathan. *The Happiness Curve: Why Life Gets Better After 50.* St. Martin's Press, 2018.

Rohr, Richard. *Falling Upward: A Spirituality for the Two Halves of Life.* Jossey-Bass, 2011.

Rowe, John Wallace, and Robert L. Kahn. *Successful Aging.* Pantheon, 1998.

Sasse, Ben. *The Vanishing American Adult: Our Coming-of-Age Crisis—and How to Rebuild a Culture of Self-Reliance.* St. Martin's Press, 2017.

Stahl, Lesley. *Becoming Grandma: The Joys and Science of the New Grandparenting.* Blue Rider Press, 2016.

Taylor, Paul. *The Next America: Boomers, Millennials, and the Looming Generational Showdown.* PublicAffairs, 2014.

Thang, Leng Leng. *Generations in Touch: Linking the Old and Young in a Tokyo Neighborhood.* Cornell University Press, 2001.

Tough, Paul. *Helping Children Succeed: What Works and Why.* Houghton Mifflin Harcourt, 2016.

Vaillant, George E. *Aging Well: Surprising Guideposts to a Happier Life from the Landmark Harvard Study of Adult Development.* Little, Brown, 2002.

——*Triumphs of Experience: The Men of the Harvard Grant Study.* Belknap Press, 2012.

Werner, Emmy, with Ruth S. Smith. *Journeys from Childhood to Midlife: Risk, Resilience, and Recovery.* Cornell University Press, 2001.

——*Overcoming the Odds: High Risk Children from Birth to Adulthood.* Cornell University Press, 1992.

——*Vulnerable Yet Invincible: A Longitudinal Study of Resilient Children and Youth.* McGraw-Hill, 1982.

Zaslow, Jeffrey, and Randy Pausch. *The Last Lecture.* Hyperion, 2008.

RECOMMENDED MOVIE LIST

Akeelah and the Bee (2006)
Cars 3 (2017)
Chapter & Verse (2015)
Cinema Paradiso (1988)
Coco (2017)
Creed (2015)
Faces Places (2017)
Finding Forrester (2000)
Good Will Hunting (1997)
Harry Potter and the Half-Blood Prince (2009)
Hunt for the Wilderpeople (2016)
Keep On Keepin' On (2014)
Late Night (2019)
Little Miss Sunshine (2006)
Million Dollar Baby (2004)
Moana (2016)
Remember the Titans (2000)
Secondhand Lions (2003)
Stand and Deliver (1988)
Star Wars: The Empire Strikes Back (1980)
The Farewell (2019)
The Intern (2015)
The Karate Kid (1984)
The Peanut Butter Falcon (2019)
To Sir, With Love (1967)
Up (2009)
War Room (2015)
Whale Rider (2002)

RECOMMENDED VIDEO LIST

Applewhite, Ashton. "Let's End Ageism." TED. April 2017. www.ted.com/talks/ashton_applewhite_let_s_end_ageism.

Brooks, David. "Should You Live for Your Résumé . . . or Your Eulogy?" TED2014, March 2014. www.ted.com/talks/david_brooks_should_you_live_for_your_resume_or_your_eulogy.

Carstensen, Laura. "Older People Are Happier." TEDxWomen. December 2011. www.ted.com/talks/laura_carstensen_older_people_are_happier.

Conley, Chip. "The Modern Elder." Wisdom 2.0. February 2017. youtu.be/7NdE0RMz0CA.

"Father Gregory Boyle on Our Deep Longing for Community." 3-Minute Storyteller. April 2018. youtu.be/i4YJp0FsUhY.

Fennelly, Carol. "2013 Purpose Prize Winner—Carol Fennelly." November 2013. youtu.be/9RkFJIXPWDk.

Freedman, Marc. "How to Live Forever." TEDxSanFrancisco. August 2017. www.tedxsanfrancisco.com/talk-marc-freedman.

Gardner, John. "Common Cause 20th Anniversary" September 1990. Part 1, youtu.be/vbNrfuwslno; Part 2, youtu.be/o0Dxz_jV4oM.

"In Easthampton Village, Everyone Helps the Children." *Boston Globe*. December 2015. www.bostonglobe.com/metro/2015/12/20/village-raise-adopted-foster-children/GoqaPeIrxsZieXd39YMPkM/story.html.

"In Seoul, Preventing Suicide by Simulating Death." *Atlantic*. May 2016. vimeo.com/162447459.

Intergenerational School. "2014 Eisner Prize Winner The Intergenerational School." November 2014. youtu.be/j_ThNx1kRzo.

Jenkins, Jo Ann. "How to Fight Back Against Age Discrimination and Create a New Vision for Aging." Dr. Phil. April 2016. youtu.be/VM5KUngQO_I.

Jobs, Steve. "Stanford Commencement Address." June 2005. youtu.be/UF8uR6Z6KLc.

Jones, Hubie. "What's Your Encore?" TakePart TV. May 2012. youtu.be/8fZntRzM1ow.

Joseph, Jamal. "2015 Purpose Prize winner—Jamal Joseph." November 2015. youtu.be/D3axJGVS1PI.

"Kareem Abdul-Jabbar on Bond with UCLA Coach John Wooden." CBS This Morning. May 2017. youtu.be/HHBwyNZRI-4.

"*Keep On Keepin' On* Official Trailer 1 (2014)—Documentary HD." Movieclips Indie. August 2014. youtu.be/kjR74w_GFWE.

Kellaway, Lucy. "I'm Becoming a Teacher at 58—This Is Why You Should Too." TEDxLondonBusinessSchool. July 2017. youtu.be/LilaqTaQ6ss.

L.A. Kitchen. "2015 Eisner Prize Winner." February 2016. youtu.be/uBSXx M8VZuU.

Meadows, Bridge. "2014 Eisner Prize Winner Bridge Meadows." November 2014. youtu.be/wdmPiC2AUfA.

Mikelson, Belle. "2015 Purpose Prize Winner—Belle Mikelson." November 2015. youtu.be/YZNaL4_yGO4.

"A Retirement Home for Young and Old." Great Big Story. September 2016. youtu.be/Y56zLb4NgSU.

"Trailer—*The Growing Season*." Documentary trailer. June 4, 2015. thegrowing-seasonfilm.com/trailer/.

Waldinger, Robert. "What Makes a Good Life? Lessons from the Longest Study in Happiness." TEDxBeaconStreet. November 2015. www.ted.com/talks/robert _waldinger_what_makes_a_good_life_lessons_from_the_longest_study _on_happiness.

Werner, Emmy. UC Davis Development & Alumni Relations. February 2015. www.youtube.com/watch?v=jzcLo-LHTms.

INDEX

Marc Freedman is CEO and president of Encore.org, an organization he founded in 1998. Freedman is a member of the *Wall Street Journal's* "Experts" group, a frequent commentator in the national media, and the author of four previous books.

Originator of the encore career idea linking second acts to the greater good, Freedman cofounded Experience Corps to mobilize people over fifty to improve the school performance and prospects of low-income elementary school students in twenty-two US cities. He also spearheaded the creation of the Encore Fellowships program, a one-year fellowship helping individuals translate their midlife skills into second acts focused on social impact, and the Purpose Prize, an annual $100,000 prize for social entrepreneurs in the second half of life (AARP now runs both Experience Corps and the Purpose Prize.)

Freedman was named a Social Entrepreneur of the Year by the Schwab Foundation and the World Economic Forum, was recognized as one of the nation's leading social entrepreneurs by *Fast Company* magazine three years in a row, and has been honored with the Skoll Award for Social Entrepreneurship. He has been a visiting fellow at Stanford University, the David and Lucile Packard Foundation, and King's College, University of London. Freedman serves or has served on the boards and advisory councils of numerous groups, including the George Warren Brown School of Social Work at Washington University in St. Louis, the Stanford University Distinguished Careers Institute, the Milken Institute's Center for the Future of Aging, and the EnCorps STEM Teachers Program.

A high honors graduate of Swarthmore College, with an MBA from the Yale School of Management, Freedman lives in the San Francisco Bay area with his wife, Leslie Gray, and their three children.

PublicAffairs is a publishing house founded in 1997. It is a tribute to the standards, values, and flair of three persons who have served as mentors to countless reporters, writers, editors, and book people of all kinds, including me.

I. F. STONE, proprietor of *I. F. Stone's Weekly*, combined a commitment to the First Amendment with entrepreneurial zeal and reporting skill and became one of the great independent journalists in American history. At the age of eighty, Izzy published *The Trial of Socrates*, which was a national bestseller. He wrote the book after he taught himself ancient Greek.

BENJAMIN C. BRADLEE was for nearly thirty years the charismatic editorial leader of *The Washington Post*. It was Ben who gave the *Post* the range and courage to pursue such historic issues as Watergate. He supported his reporters with a tenacity that made them fearless and it is no accident that so many became authors of influential, best-selling books.

ROBERT L. BERNSTEIN, the chief executive of Random House for more than a quarter century, guided one of the nation's premier publishing houses. Bob was personally responsible for many books of political dissent and argument that challenged tyranny around the globe. He is also the founder and longtime chair of Human Rights Watch, one of the most respected human rights organizations in the world.

· · ·

For fifty years, the banner of Public Affairs Press was carried by its owner Morris B. Schnapper, who published Gandhi, Nasser, Toynbee, Truman, and about 1,500 other authors. In 1983, Schnapper was described by *The Washington Post* as "a redoubtable gadfly." His legacy will endure in the books to come.

Peter Osnos, *Founder*